LEARN & PLAY
GUITAR

INCLUDES VIDEO LESSONS

First Edition - 2025

Copyright © Pauric Mather - All Rights Reserved.

No part of this publication may be reproduced in any form or by any means graphic, electronic, or mechanical, including photocopying, recording, taping, or information storage and retrieval systems - without the prior written permission of the author.

ISBN-13: 979-8289092144

Layout & Design
Hammad Khalid - Malaysia - *HMDPublishing.com*

Cover Design
PixelStudio - Bosnia and Herzegovina

Translation
Florica Dohan - Ireland

Photography
Emma Curtin - Ireland

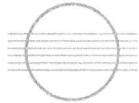

LearnAndPlayGuitar.com

LEARN & PLAY GUITAR

The ability to play guitar is **"A Priceless Gift"**. It lets your heart speak, and your imagination roam. Even when words fail, music speaks. And yet, unlike material wealth, once you have it, no one can take it away from you.

The lessons in this book have helped thousands of people to play guitar. They are the most complete, individual and personalised you will ever find. You start simply by knowing what not to do - and also by making sure you have the right guitar to learn on.

From there, it is vital that you follow each lesson step by step. Don't just read them. Personalise and interact with them. Highlight tips that really transform your guitar playing.

MAKE THIS ... **YOUR OWN BOOK**

Do not skip lessons. The only way they will not work is if you're too eager to move to the next lesson. By taking the time to absorb what you just learned, the quality of your guitar playing will be so much better. And you can achieve in weeks, what took many people years to learn.

So Come On Now ... **Pick Up Your Guitar** ... and come with me on

A Truly Unique Musical Journey!

CONTENTS

Learn & Play Guitar	3
How Not To Play Guitar	6
The Best Guitar For You	10
How To Tune Your Guitar	12
Start At Perfect	14
How To Hold A Guitar Pick	16
How To Position Your Chord Hand	18
The Best Way To Learn Guitar Chords	20
How To Read Chord Diagrams	22
5 Easy Guitar Chords	24
2 Playing Exercises	30
How To Play Rhythm Guitar	32
How To Roll Guitar Rhythms	34
6 Popular Guitar Rhythms	36
How To Change Chords Fast	38
4 New Chords	40
How To Use A Capo	44
2 Playing Exercises	46
The Spider Exercise	48
3 Easy Chord Changes	52
2 Playing Exercises	56

How To Time Guitar Rhythms	58
4 New Chords	60
4 Playing Exercises	64
2 New Chords	68
More Easy Chord Changes	70
8 Playing Exercises	71
How To Read Guitar Tablature	82
How To Play Fingerstyle Guitar	84
6 Popular Fingerstyles	86
Romanza - Fingerstyle	88
3 New Chords	90
4 Playing Exercises	93
2 New Chords	98
6 Playing Exercises	100
More About G Chord	108
How To Play F Chord	110
4 Playing Exercises	112
2 New Chords	116
6 Playing Exercises	118
2 New Chords	124
2 Playing Exercises	126
Chord Index	128
Meet The Author	130

HOW *NOT* TO PLAY GUITAR

There are 8 reasons why people fail to learn guitar. Avoid them and you have just about written your own guarantee of success. Here they are;

- Weak fingers
- Bad guitar teachers
- Bad thumb positioning
- Learning rhythms badly
- Learning G the wrong way
- Holding a guitar pick badly
- Learning on nylon string guitars
- Holding guitar neck in chord hand

BAD THUMB

If your thumb is badly positioned your guitar will often sound muddy.

If you raise your knuckle, you can play basic chords. But fast chord changing is impossible.

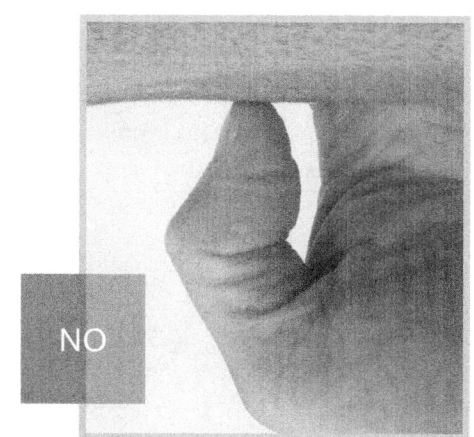

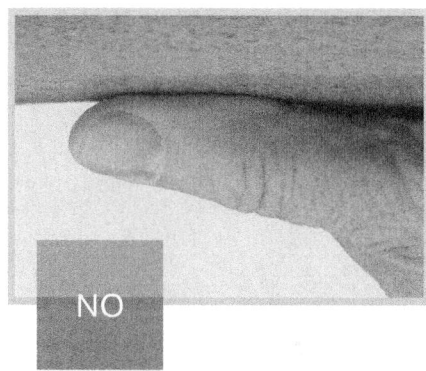

If your thumb falls sideways, It makes it very difficult to change chords quickly, and to play chords up the guitar neck.

 ## BAD HOLD

With a bad grip you can play basic rhythms but you will find advanced rhythms very difficult to perfect.

Learning the G chord as shown below is one of the main reasons why people give up playing guitar. This G only works when you pick each string one by one. But not when you strum all the strings at once. It sounds muddy. And it can lead to other problems as you try to improve.

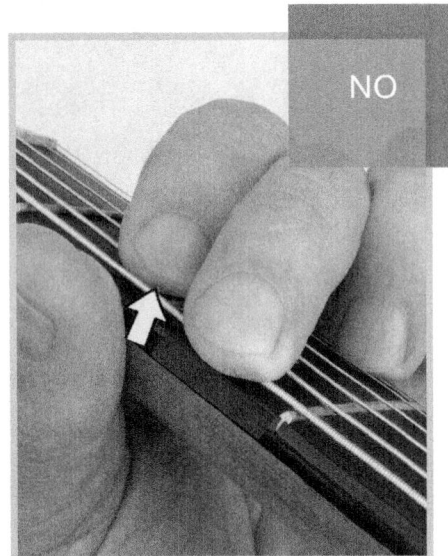

Changing to C and D can be difficult.

You can't add as many bass runs or ornamentation.

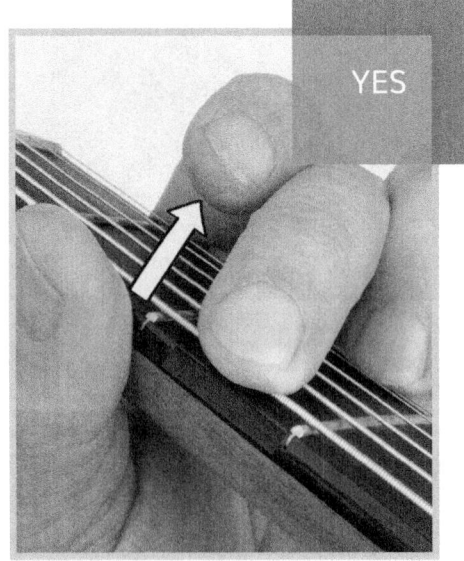

The best way to learn G is more difficult, but only for a few weeks. After that you have a lifetime of endless possibilities. It is mostly played two ways.

One gives a rich airy sound. The other frees your 1st and 2nd fingers to add more notes, polychords, and bass runs.

Most beginners pull the guitar neck back and crouch out and down to see the strings. Avoid this and you will learn and improve much much faster. And your guitar will be so much easier to play.

Guitar neck pulled back too far

- A faulty set up closes many doors
- It makes chord changing very difficult
- It makes strumming guitar rhythms very difficult
- It also can block the air supply needed to sing well

THE BEST GUITAR FOR YOU

If you're a beginner you need to know if you strum better with your right or left hand. The one you write with is almost always the hand you strum a guitar with. If you're not sure try strumming a guitar both ways to see which is most natural.

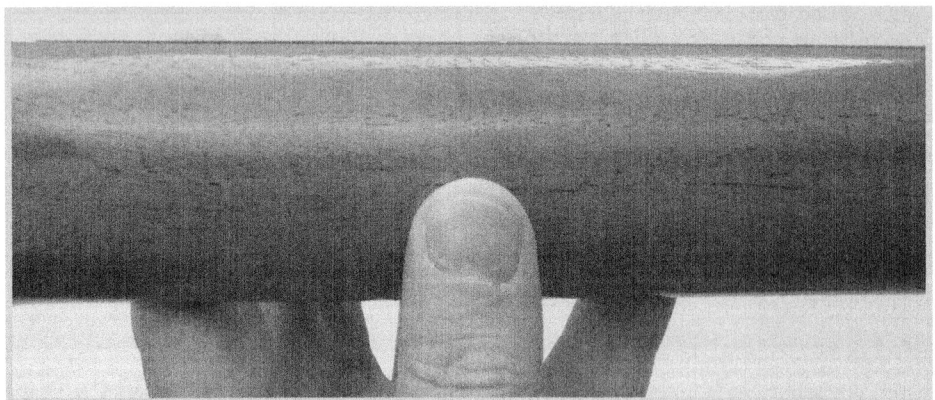

A slim neck

Most professionals play slim neck - steel string - acoustic guitars. So should you (unless you want to play classical guitar).

Light gauge strings are easier to play and won't hurt your fingertips too much. By keeping a guitar in a case when not practicing the strings can last for a year or more.

If it's left out they tend to gather dust and need to be replaced often. You can also wipe them after playing.

 **GIRLS**

Many of you have smaller body frames than men so it makes more sense to learn on a slim size and slim neck guitar.

As well as being much easier to play, you will be much more comfortable.

HOW TO TUNE YOUR GUITAR

Guitar tuners can be tricky for beginners to use. Because they process sound waves you have to pick a string to bring it alive. Then you need to keep sounding the string to keep it responding....and turn the tuning head at the same time to tune the string.

A guitar tuner can process only one sound at a time. If it hears more it doesn't know which sound to process and gets confused.

A clip-on guitar tuner will solve all these problems instantly. They are the most user friendly of all tuners because they only work when attached to the guitar head. So they hear your guitar and nothing else. You can even tune with it in very noisy or crowded areas.

Clip-on guitar tuner

STRING	NOTE
6th	E
5th	A
4th	D
3rd	G
2nd	B
1st	E

It's not enough to centre a needle or get a green light. The note on your tuner must match the string you are tuning. Sometimes the strings need to be tuned more than once. After tuning it's a good idea to strum a little to settle them. Then tune them again and you're ready to play.

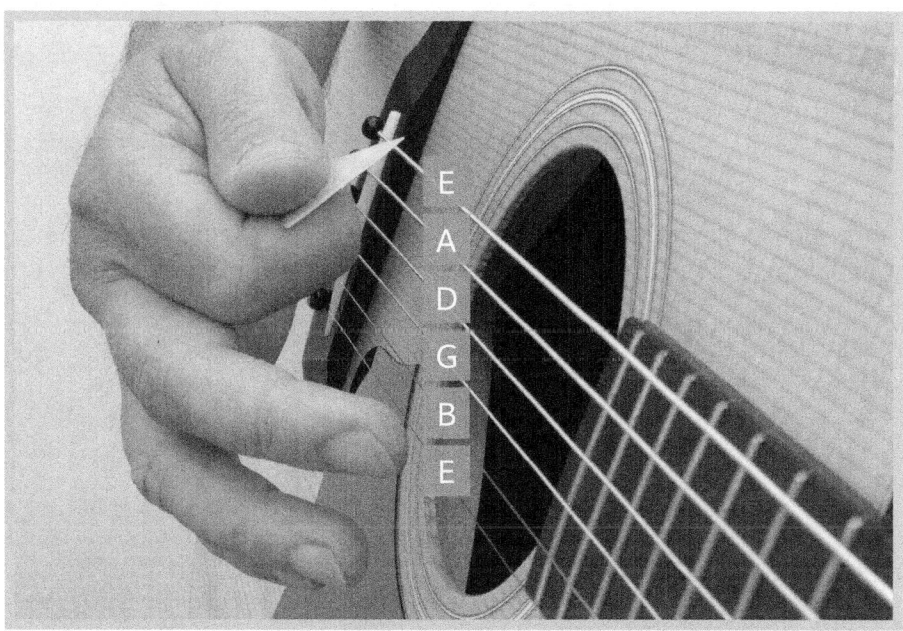

START AT PERFECT

How you set up to play guitar has a huge impact on how quickly you learn. Neglect this vital starting point and it's much more difficult to play.

It only takes a few minutes to learn, but you greatly increase your chances of success.

And if you learn to hold a guitar pick correctly from the start, it's much easier to learn rhythms.

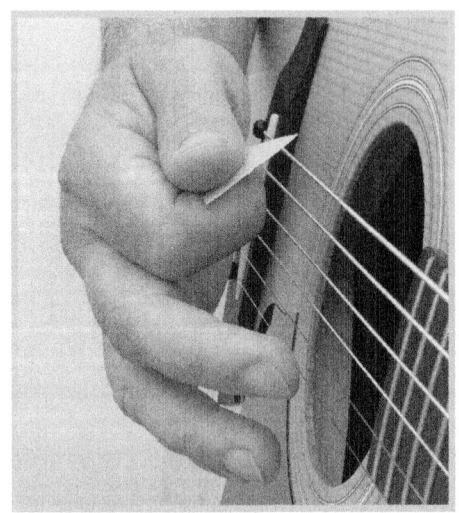

Hold guitar pick correctly

Guitar rests on the same leg as your rhythm hand

Keep the guitar neck angled out about the length of your forearm. This sets your hand in front of you, the same as turning a key in a door. It makes chord changing much easier, and helps to release your natural ability.

Also, the top of the guitar is tilted towards you. Now you can easily see all six strings.

HOW TO HOLD A GUITAR PICK

Some people don't like using a guitar pick. They say it slips as soon as they start playing.

But in reality it's their fingers that lose position because they're not holding it the right way.

The learning technique on the next page gives you a great way to hold a guitar pick.

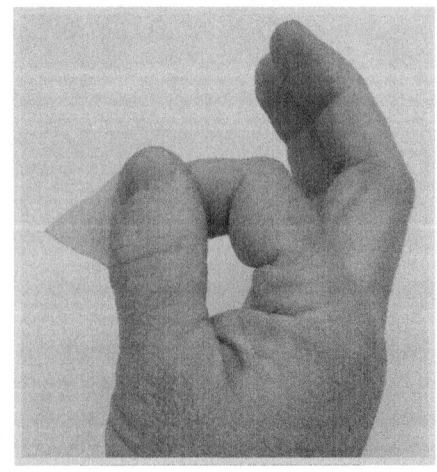

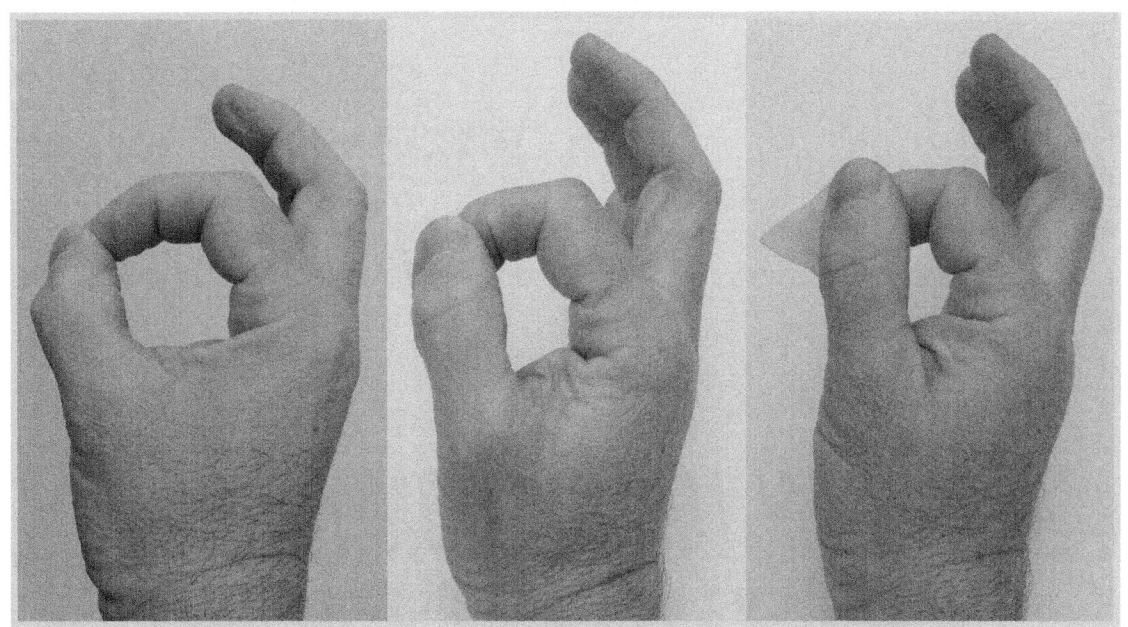

Make a circle | Slide finger under thumb | Add guitar pick

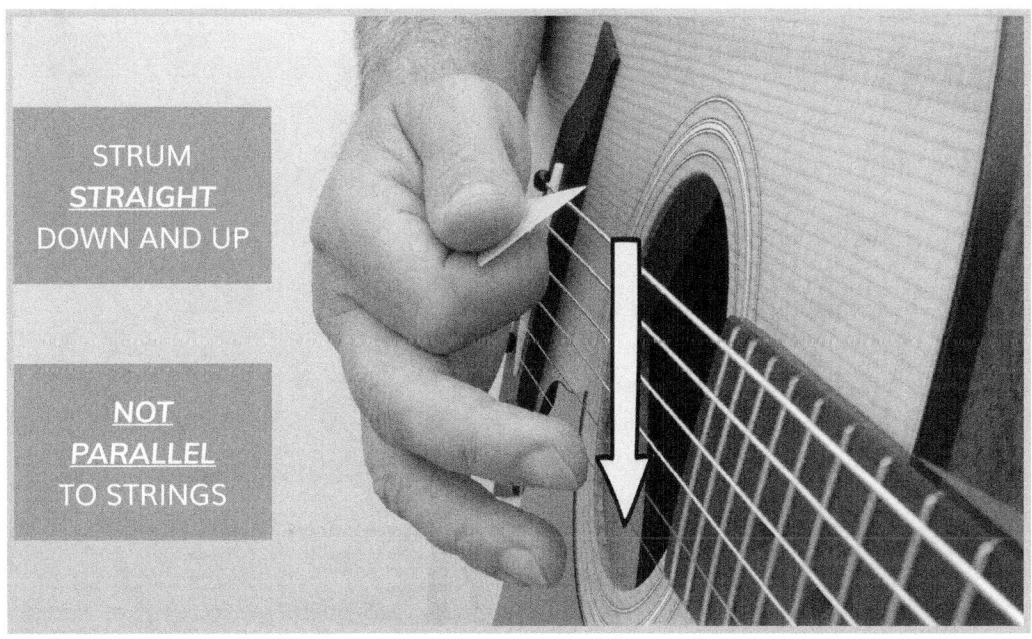

STRUM **STRAIGHT** DOWN AND UP

NOT PARALLEL TO STRINGS

HOW TO POSITION YOUR CHORD HAND

Here is the simplest and best way to position your chord hand every time:

1. Tilt your guitar
2. Position your thumb
3. Then position your fingers

This simple approach makes it much easier to learn guitar chords. And it's easier to speed up your chord changing too, which is the great secret of playing guitar.

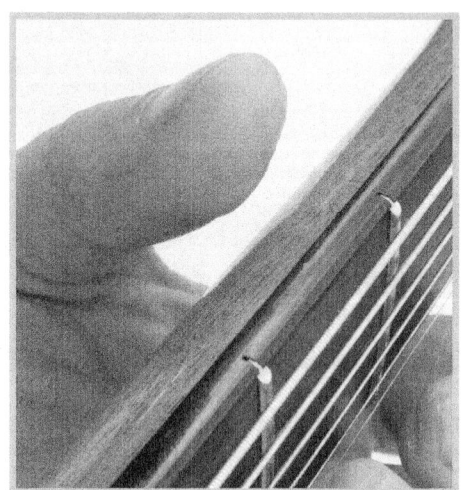

Thumb first - Then fingers

1 TILT YOUR GUITAR

Tilting makes learning chords so much easier. The guitar is now doing some of the work for you. It also helps to produce a good sound.

2 POSITION YOUR THUMB

Thumb on top for open chords

Thumb low and centred for barre chords

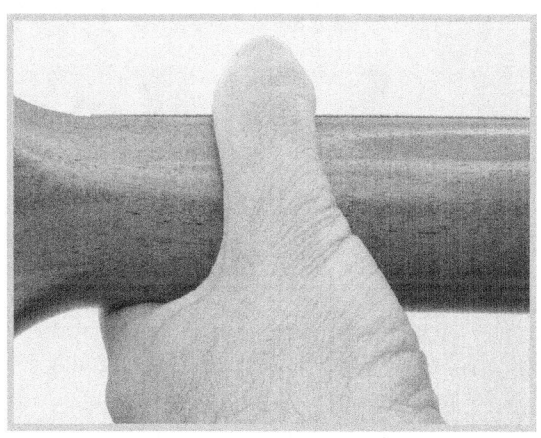

3 POSITION YOUR FINGERS

The simple 3 step approach here is technically perfect and exactly as played by top guitarists.

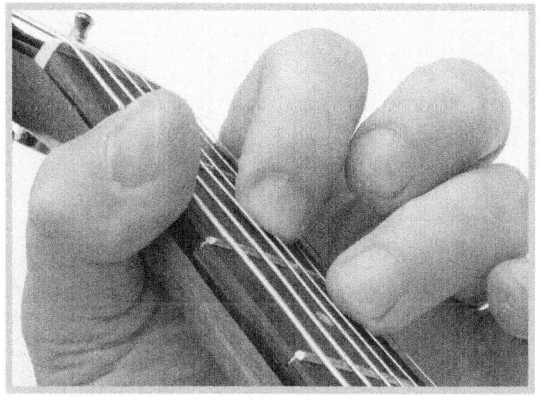

THE BEST WAY TO LEARN CHORDS

The absolute best way to learn guitar chords is to practice a sequence of 3 or 4 chords at a time. And with your chord hand only. Once you get to know the chords you can then add your rhythm hand.

As well as learning new chords, this helps to speed up your chord changes (the bit between them). Whether you're a beginner or professional, D is D and G is G. But the professional is much faster between chords.

Players' view

 # THE SECRET

Here is one of the great secrets of playing guitar. In fact without it, nothing is possible.

If you watch any great guitarist, in any style of music, anywhere in the world you'll see **"The Guitar Triangle"**.

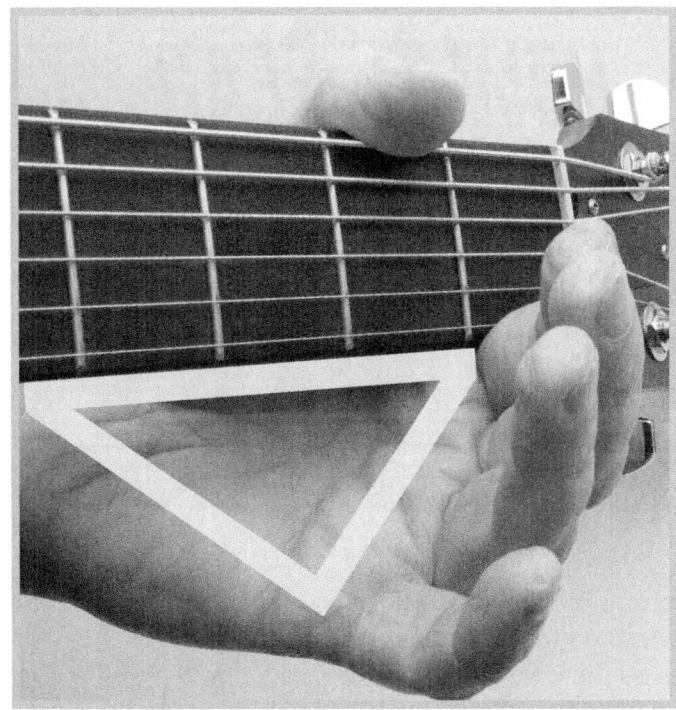

- Makes room for fingers to move
- Lets you play with your fingertips
- Prevents knuckles from collapsing
- Makes chord changing easier
- **NOT** suitable for barre chords

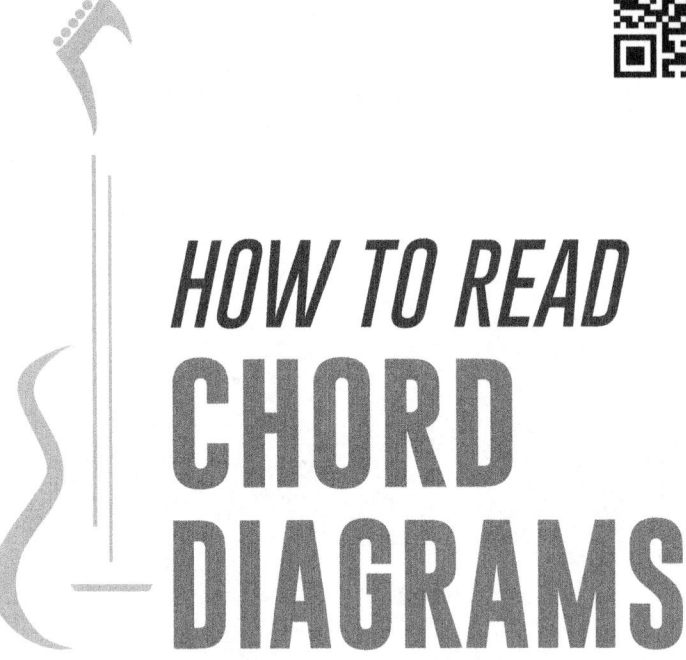

HOW TO READ CHORD DIAGRAMS

Chord diagrams are hugely helpful if you're an experienced guitarist. But because they only show you the front of the guitar neck, They do not work for most beginners.

However, if you're a beginner the secret is to combine **"The 3 Step Approach"** (Page 19) with the chord diagram.

Now they're much easier to follow - and save you time.

 Thumb

 1st Finger

 2nd Finger

 3rd Finger

 4th Finger

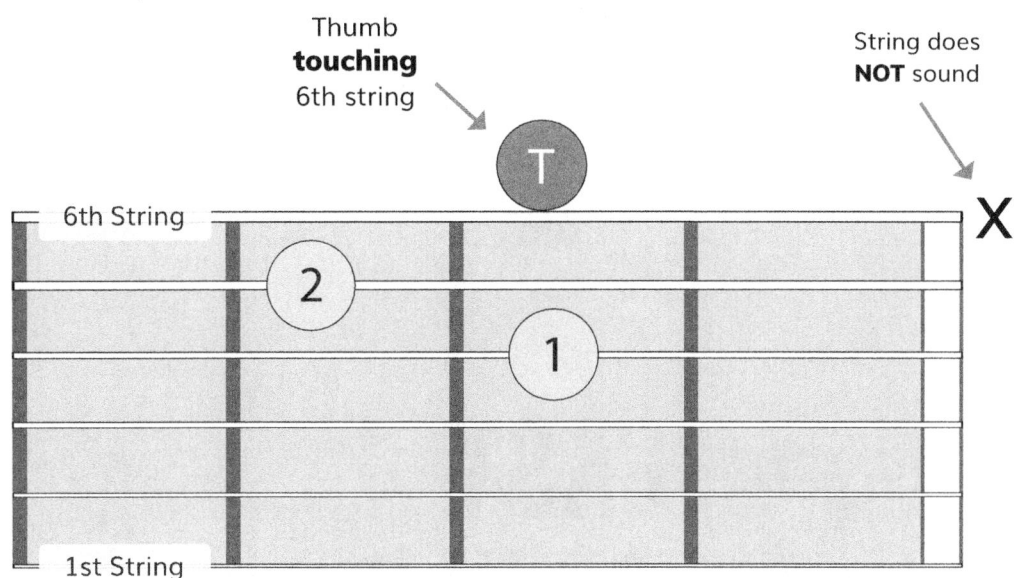

5 EASY GUITAR CHORDS

E_m

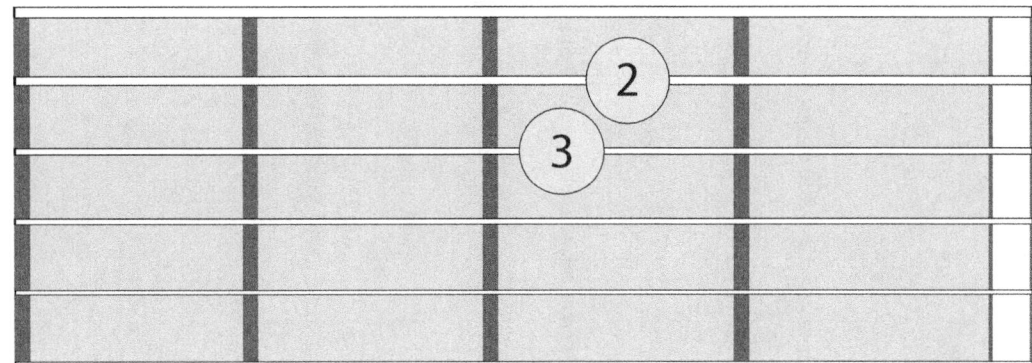

- Thumb not touching 6th string
- Can also be played with 1st and 2nd finger
- Strum 6 strings - All 6 sound

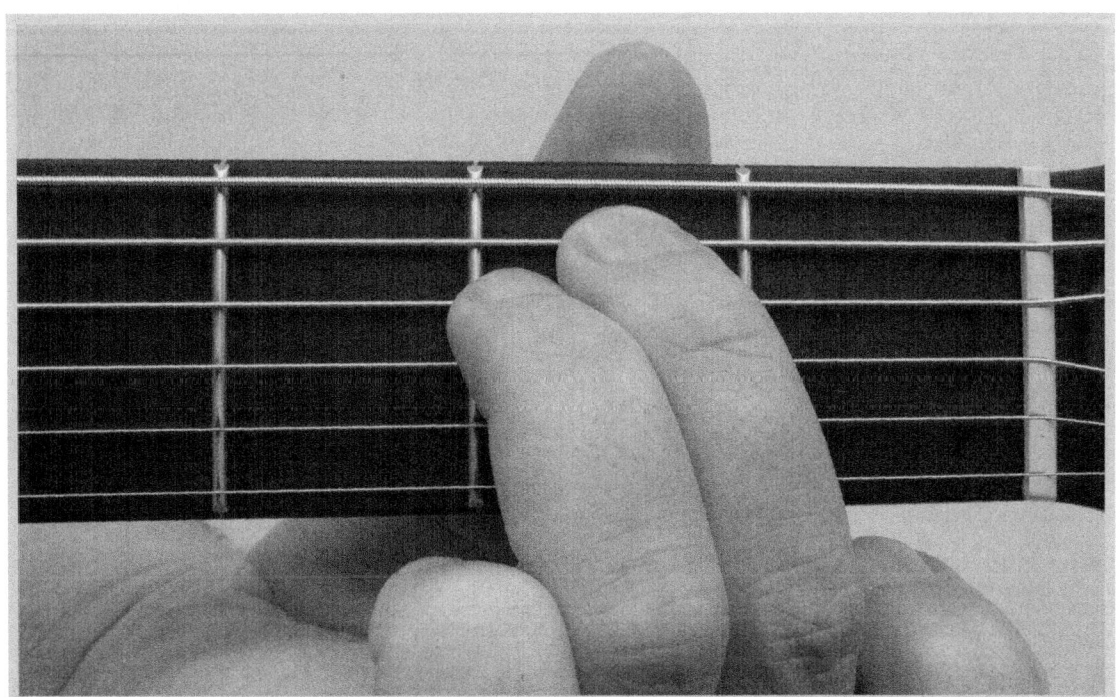

Cmaj7

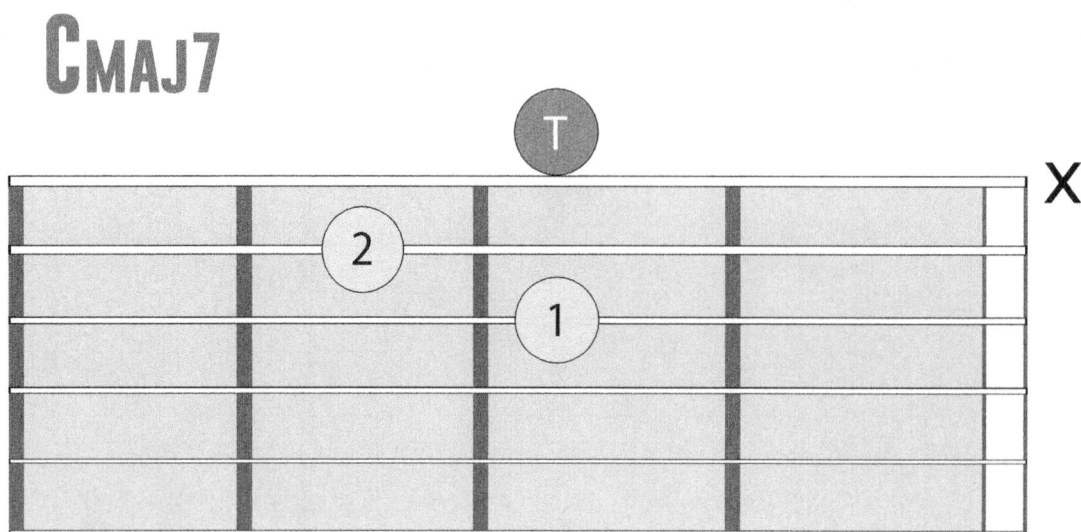

- Thumb touching 6th string
- 2nd finger in middle of fret
- Strum 6 strings - Only 5 sound

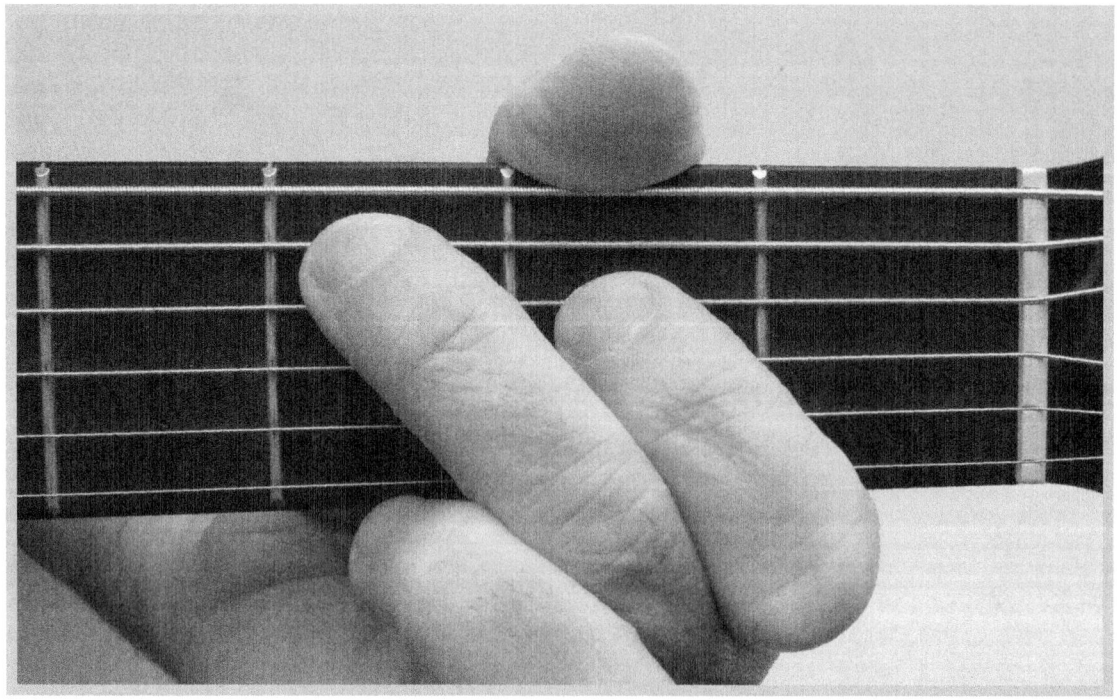

G6

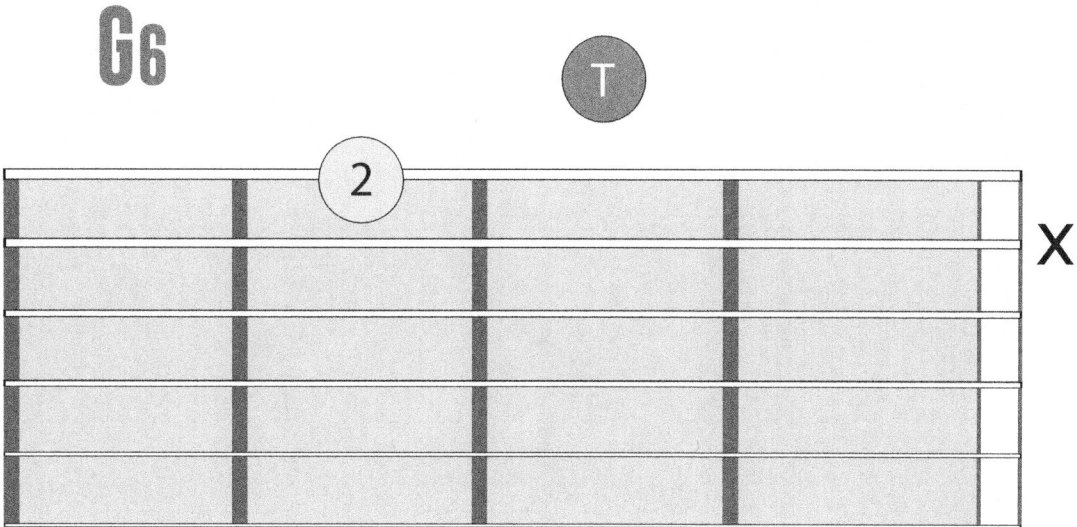

- Thumb not touching 6th string
- 5th string muted by inside of 2nd finger
- Strum 6 strings - Only 5 sound

F# EASY

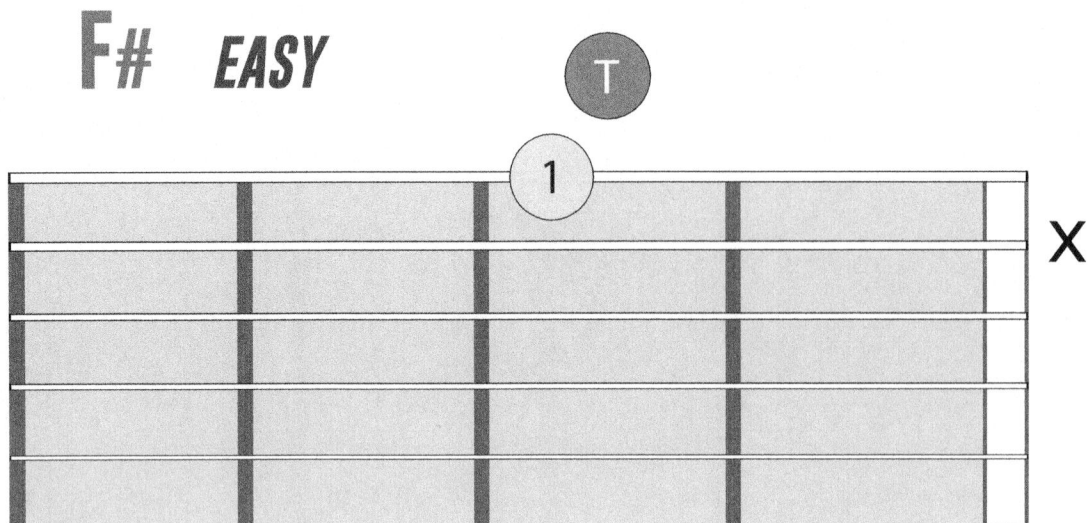

- Thumb not touching 6th string
- 5th string muted by inside of 1st finger
- Strum 6 strings - Only 5 sound

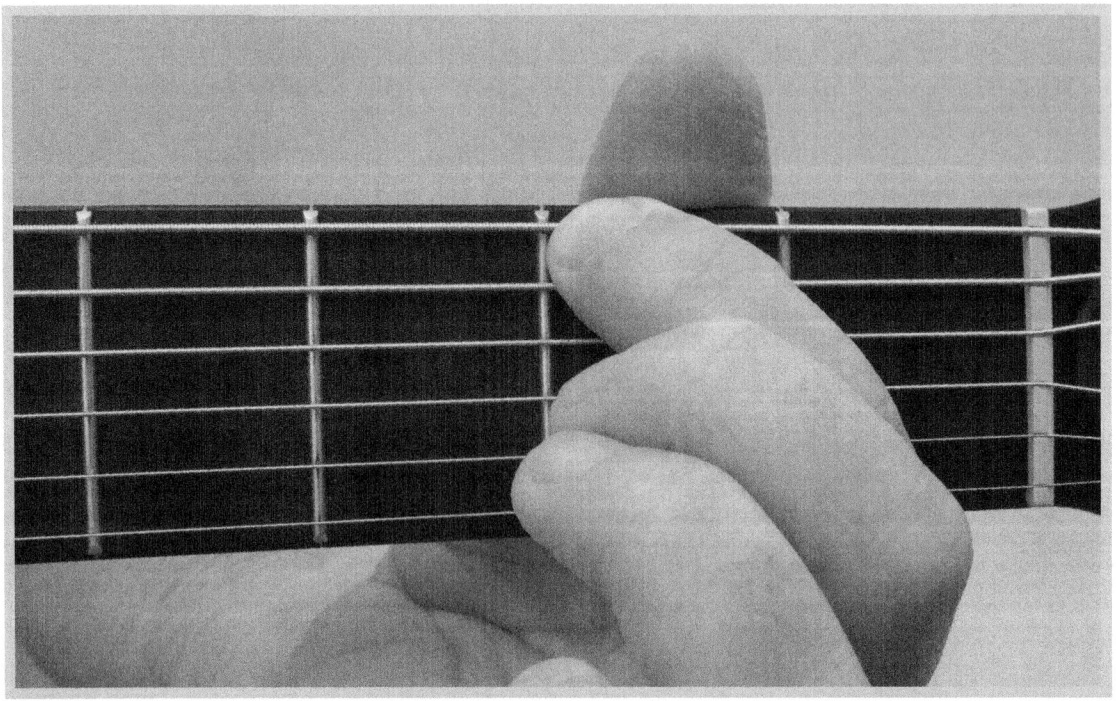

E7sus4

- Thumb not touching 6th string
- Can also be played with 1st and 2nd finger
- Strum 6 strings - All 6 sound

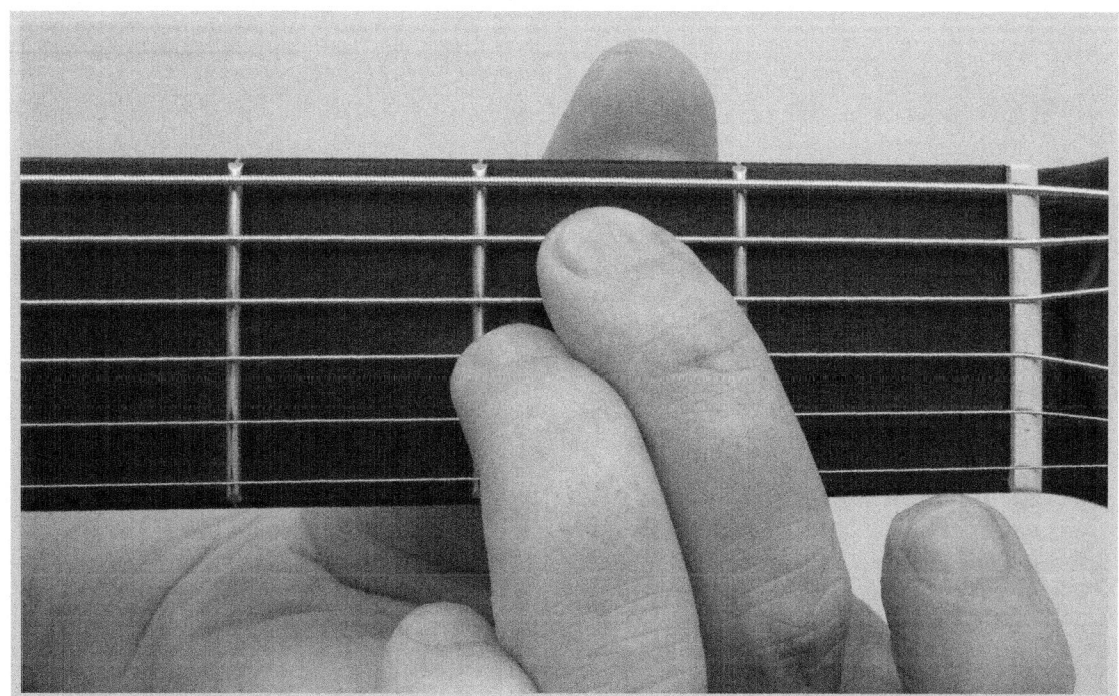

PLAYING EXERCISE

SONG EXAMPLE
Zombie - *The Cranberries*

Em
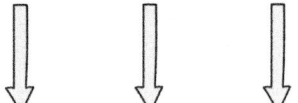 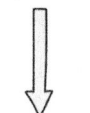    

Cmaj7
  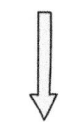    

G6
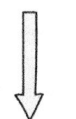       

F#
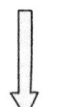    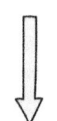   

Keep repeating this chord sequence

PLAYING EXERCISE

 **SONG EXAMPLE**
A Horse With No Name - America

Em

E7sus4

    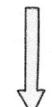 

Em

E7sus4

Keep repeating this chord sequence

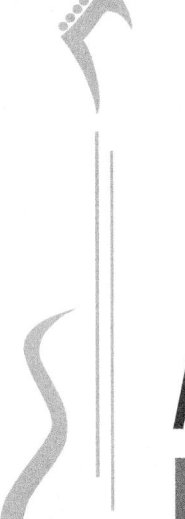

HOW TO PLAY
RHYTHM GUITAR

The quickest way to master guitar rhythms is to mute the strings with your chord hand. Now you don't have the pressure of trying to play a song at the same time.

Strumming from over the soundhole gives you a smoother sound. And because the strings seem to bend easier the pick is less lightly to slip.

Some guitarists don't use a pick at all. Instead they strum with their thumb (downstrokes) and 1st finger (upstrokes), or their first finger only for up and down strokes.

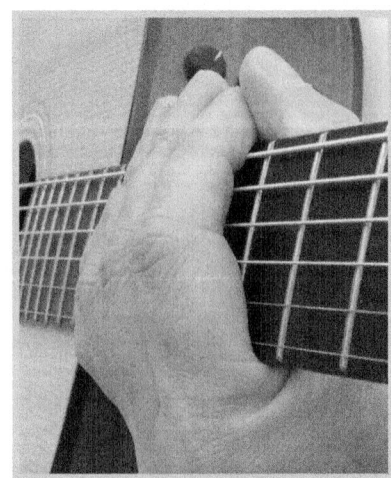

Mute the strings

PLAY FROM YOUR SHOULDERS

DOWNSTROKE

Plectrum pointed *UP*
Strum 6 strings or less

⬇ **Strum Down**
Sound The Strings

 **Strum Down**
Miss The Strings

⬆ **Strum Up**
Sound The Strings

 **Strum Up**
Miss The Strings

UPSTROKE

Plectrum pointed *DOWN*
Strum bottom 4 strings or less

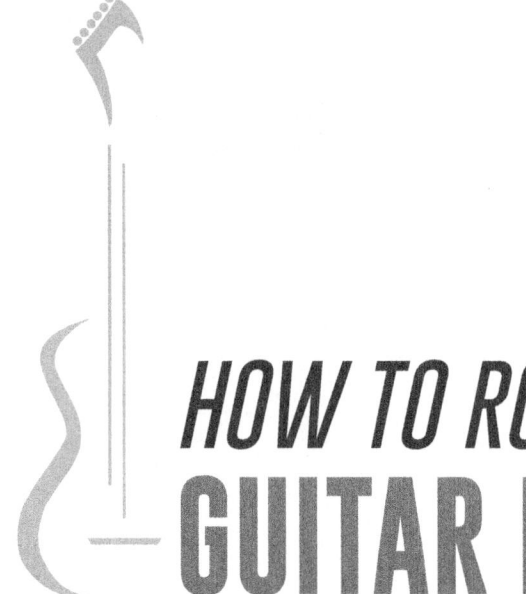

HOW TO ROLL
GUITAR RHYTHMS

To strum on time you need to softly roll your rhythms. It is the great key to good sound and perfect timing. Even though there are thousands of different sounding rhythms, there is only one pattern for them all. Here it is.

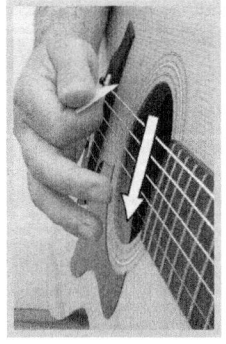

Down

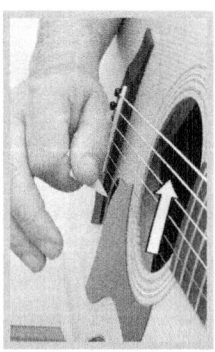

Up

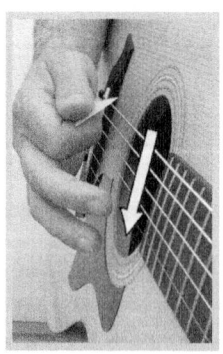

Down

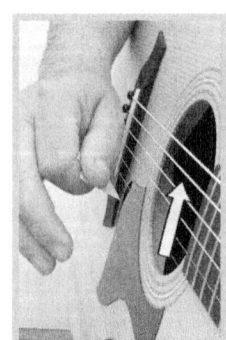

Up

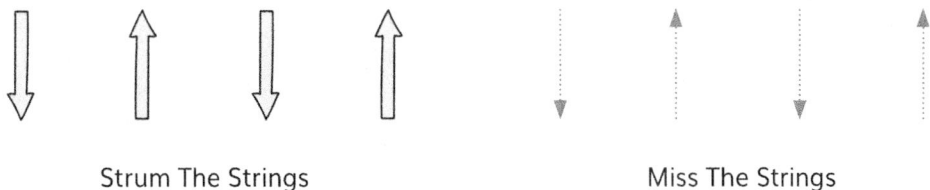

Strum The Strings Miss The Strings

Once a song starts can you feel how it rolls along? It doesn't start stop start stop. To do this on guitar your hand must have a down up down up non stop rolling movement.

In many guitar lessons, someone trying to teach you will say go down down down down. This is very misleading for many people. If I do four downstrokes in a row my hand will hit the ground.

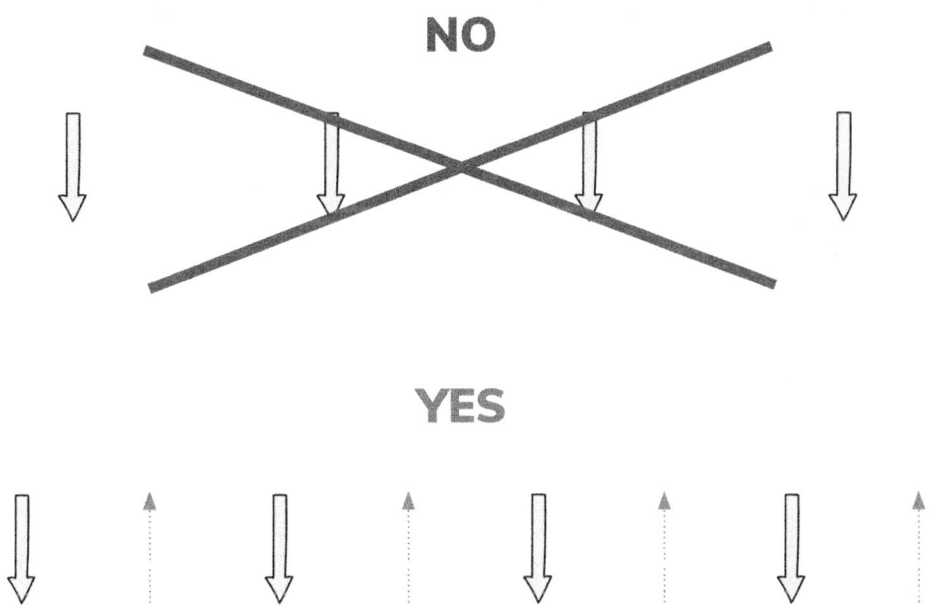

To do four downstrokes:

- You must also do upstrokes between them
- You continually roll your arm / wrist up and down
- But your audience only hears the black arrows

6 POPULAR GUITAR RHYTHMS

🎸 RHYTHM 1

↓ ↑ ↓ ↑ ↓ ↑ ↓ ↑
1   2   3   4

🎸 RHYTHM 2

↓ ↑ ↓ ↑ ↑ ↑ ↓ ↑
1   2   3   4

RHYTHM 3

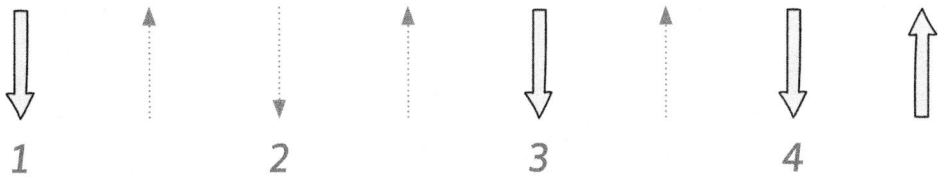

RHYTHM 4

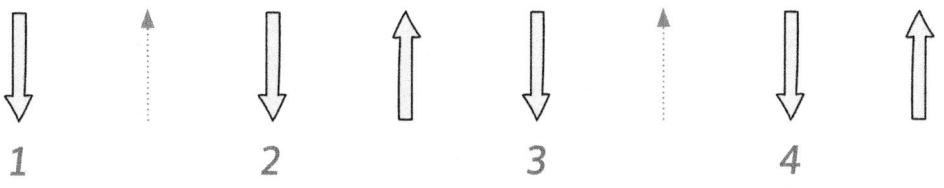

RHYTHM 5

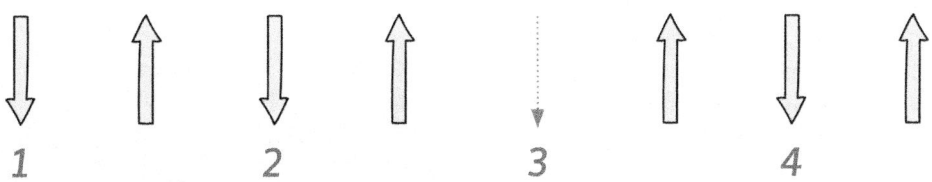

RHYTHM 6

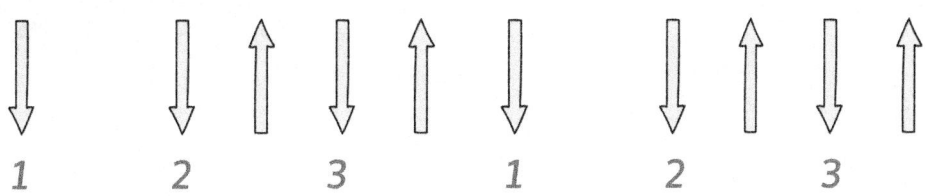

HOW TO CHANGE CHORDS FAST

When a finger is in the same position for a sequence of two or more chords you don't need to move it.

It's called a pivot finger. Just keep it pressed down and pivot around it.

Most easy chord changes have a pivot finger. Difficult ones don't. Learning guitar is much easier if you practice pivot finger changes first.

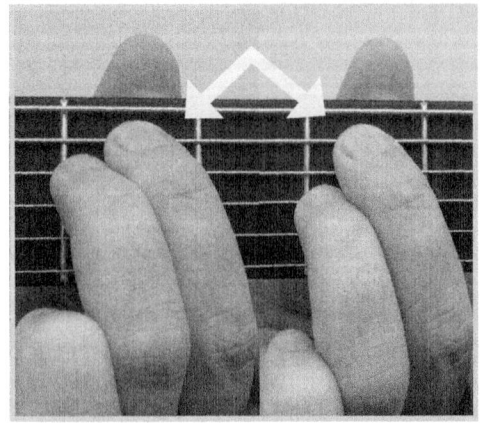

PLAYING TIP

To change chords well, start moving your fingers in the direction of the new chord, during the last upstroke of your present chord.

If you don't do this you will have a muddy sound at the start of the next chord you play.

Get it right and two things happen;

1 The chord change is easier

2 The sound Is much clearer.

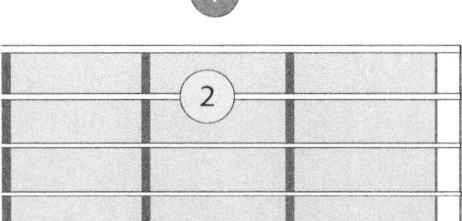

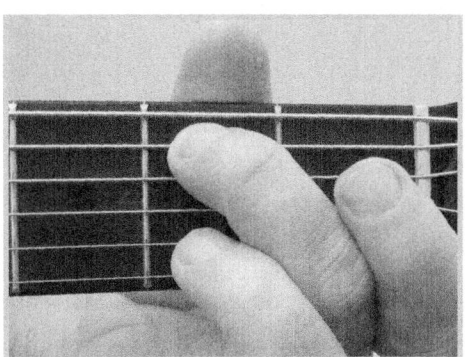

Lift 3rd finger

EM

⬇ ⬇ ⬇ ⬆ ⬇ ⬆

↑
Lift 3rd finger
↓

E7sus4

⬇ ⬇ ⬇ ⬆ ⬇ ⬆

G

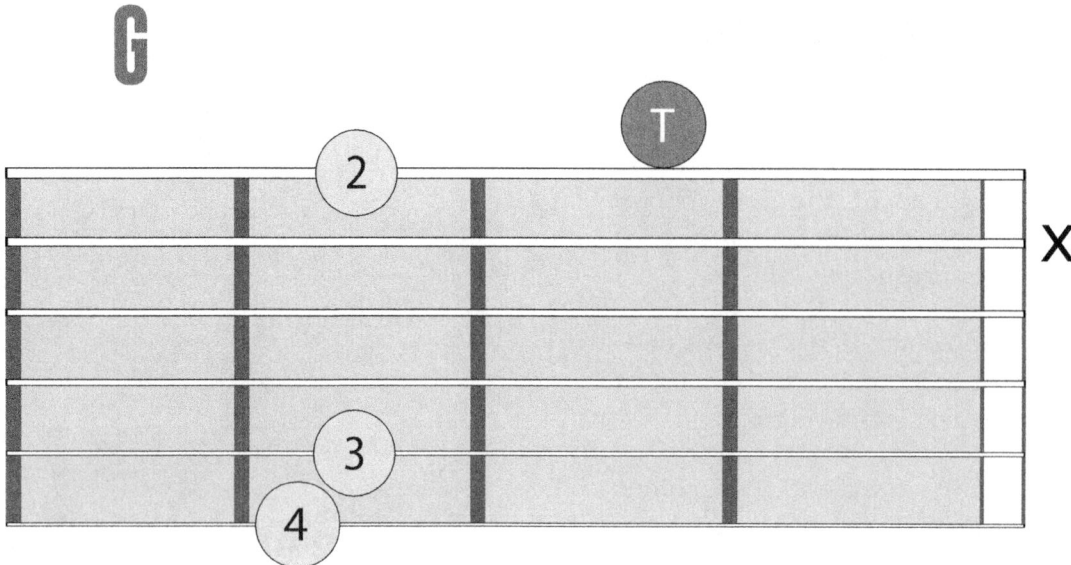

- Thumb may or may not touch 6th string
- 5th string muted by inside of 2nd finger
- Strum 6 strings - Only 5 sound

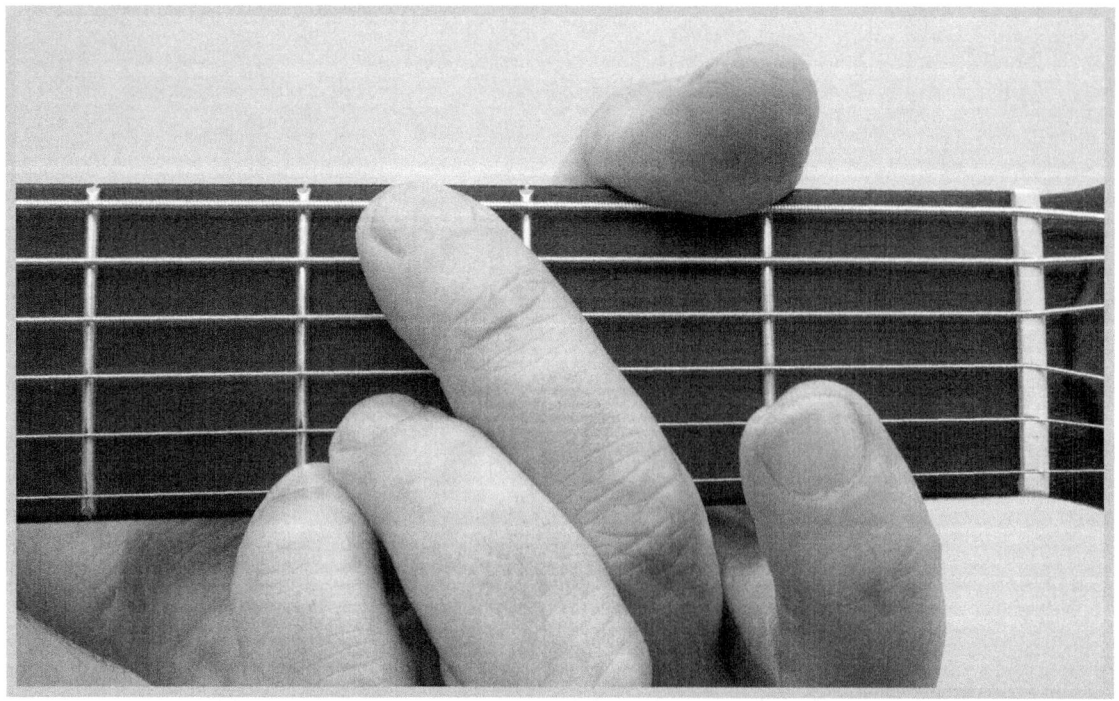

D

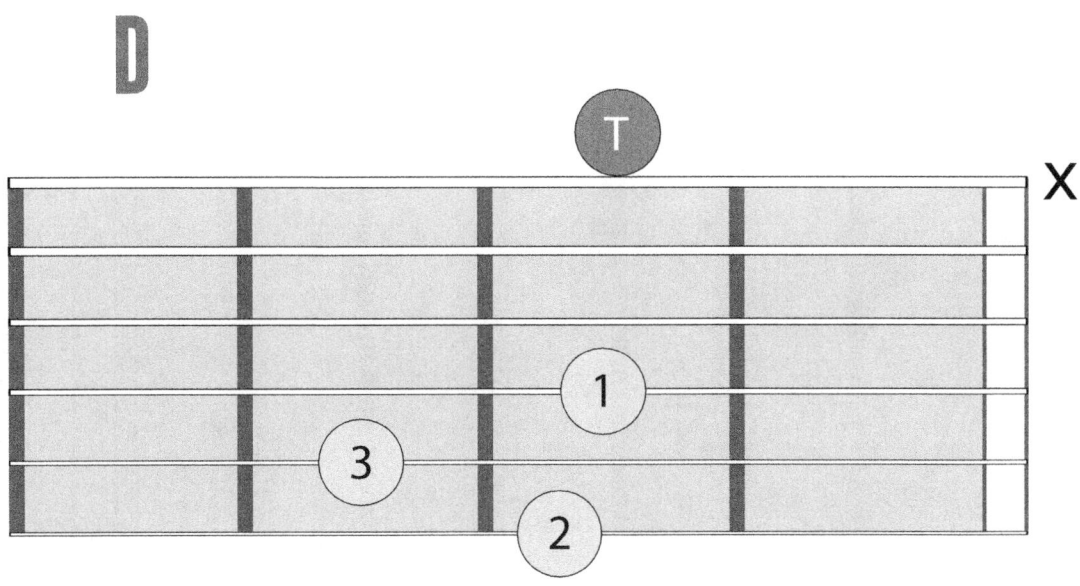

- Thumb touching 6th string
- 3rd finger in middle of fret
- Strum 6 strings - Only 5 sound

Cadd9

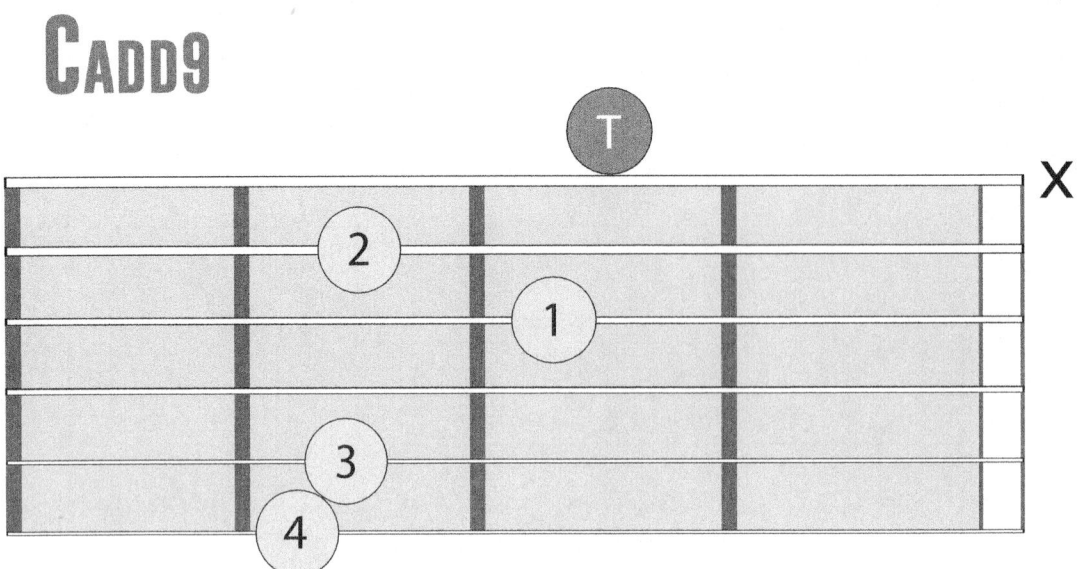

- Thumb touching 6th string
- 3rd finger in middle of fret
- Strum 6 strings - Only 5 sound

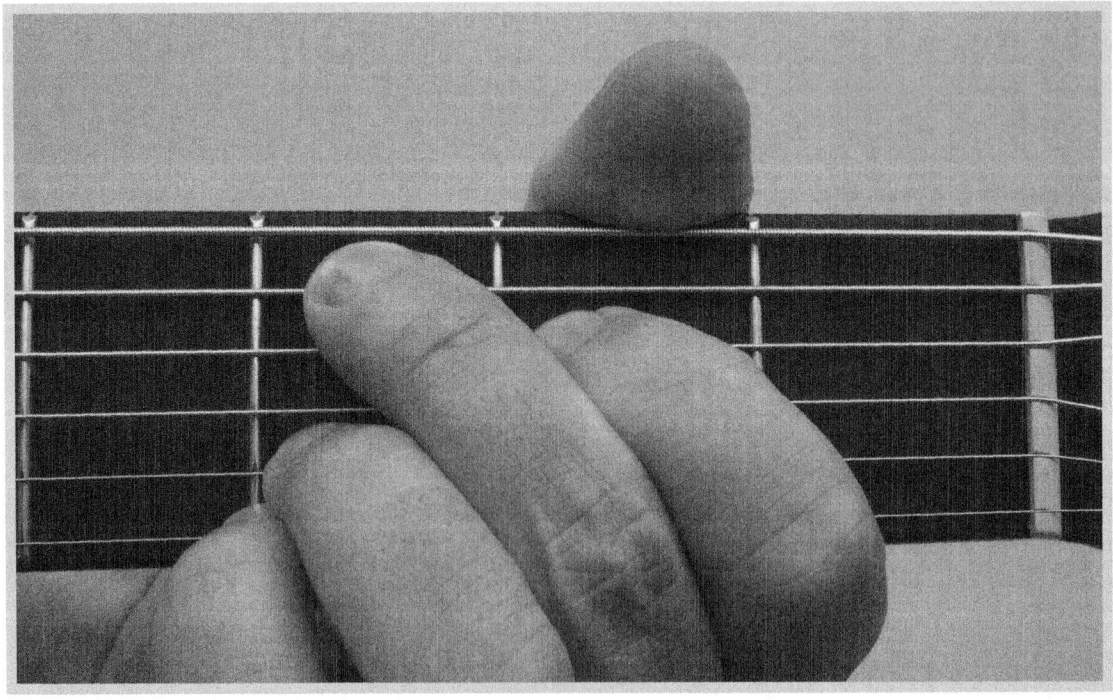

Cadd9 *

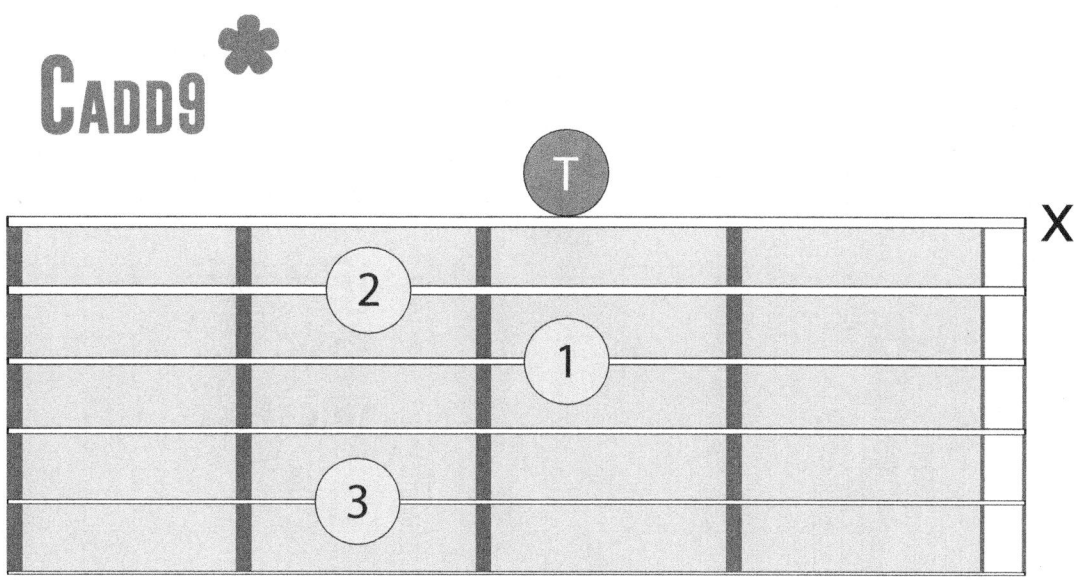

- Sometimes played instead of C
- Thumb touching 6th string
- Strum 6 strings - Only 5 sound

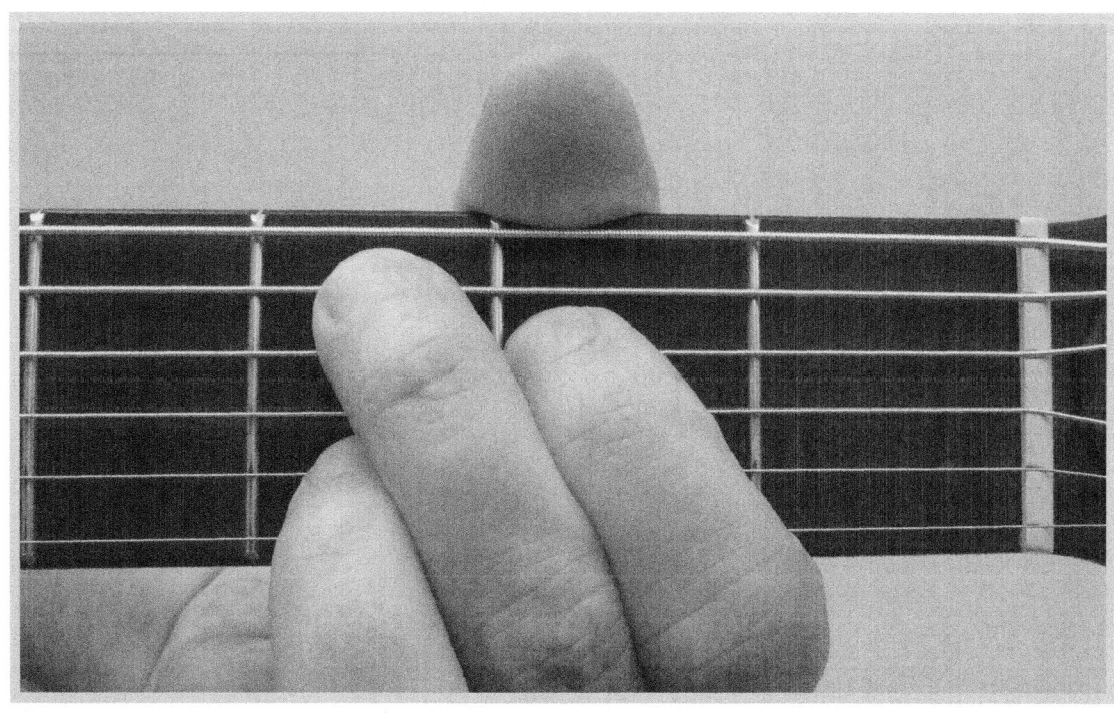

HOW TO USE A CAPO

A capo can be placed on up to ten frets. Even though you play with the same chord positions, you get a different set of sounds for each fret that the capo is on.

Also the guitar should be pitched to the vocalist in order to retain the quality of their voice.

If a song suits your voice that's great. If it doesn't, try putting a capo on the 1st fret.

All you have to do is play the same chord sequence again and the song is in a higher key.

If this position suits your voice that's great. If not you can move it up or down as many frets as you like until it suits.

Capo on 1st fret

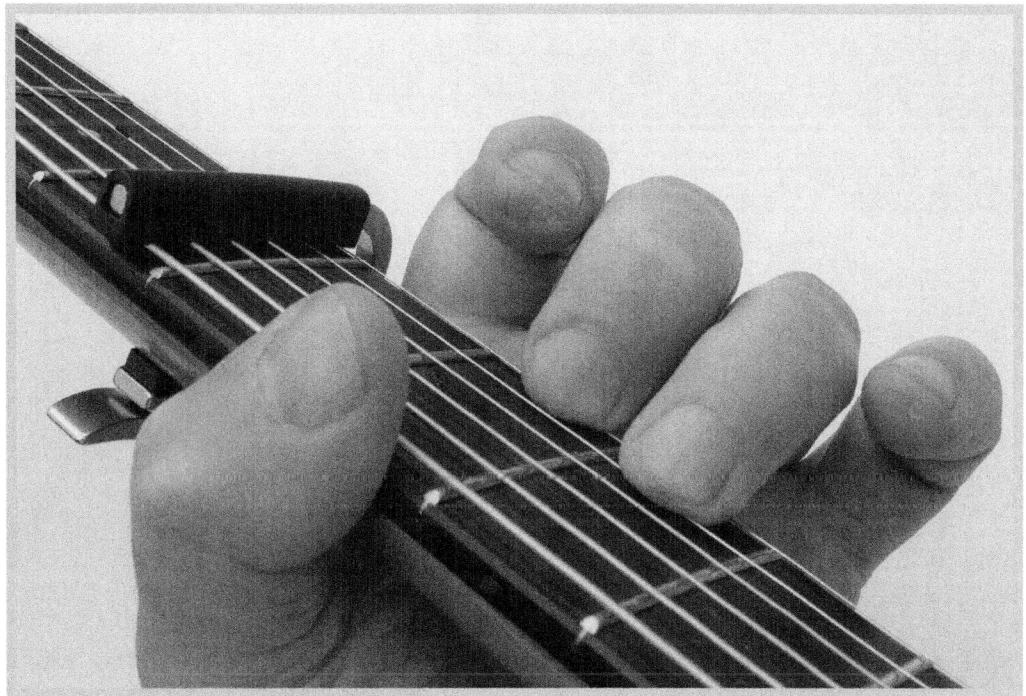

Capo on 4th fret

PLAYING EXERCISE

 SONG EXAMPLE
Time Will Tell - *Bob Marley*

CAPO ON 2ND FRET

G

CADD9

G

CADD9

Keep repeating this chord sequence

PLAYING EXERCISE

SONG EXAMPLE
Waiting In Vain - *Bob Marley*

CAPO ON 1ST FRET

G6

G6

Cmaj7

Cmaj7

Keep repeating this chord sequence

THE SPIDER EXERCISE

If you're a beginner your fingertips are too soft to produce clear sound. It usually takes about three weeks for them to harden. Secondly you need four skilled fingers. This exercise will help you to quickly upskill and strengthen all your fingers.

In everyday life you use your thumb and first two fingers for most activities. The 3rd and 4th are seldom used except maybe for typing or playing a piano. Even then you're only lightly touching the keys. Pressing guitar strings is very demanding on all four of your fingers.

STEP 1

Move 1st finger to the 5th string 1st fret

 ## STEP 2

Move 2nd finger to the 5th string 2nd fret

 ## STEP 3

Move 3rd finger to the 5th string 3rd fret

 ## STEP 4

Move 4th finger to the 5th string 4th fret

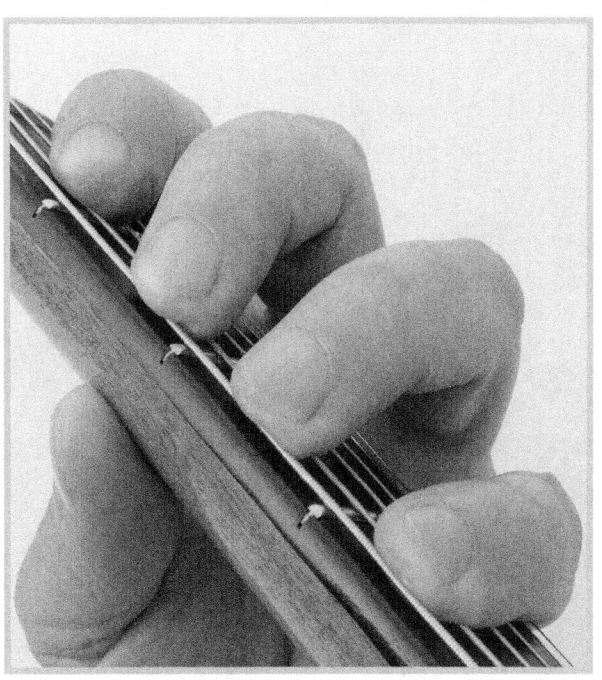

- Place 4 fingers on the 6th string
- One finger in each fret
- Move one finger at a time

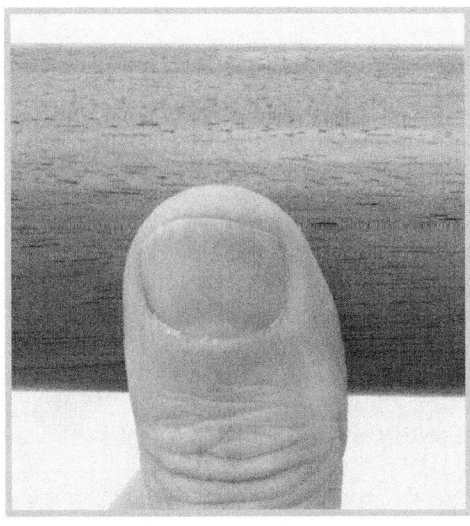

You'll find it quite difficult to move the third finger on its own. Because it's still too weak to play guitar, you might have to use your other hand to move it.

Each time you do this exercise you're a step closer to playing guitar really well.

1

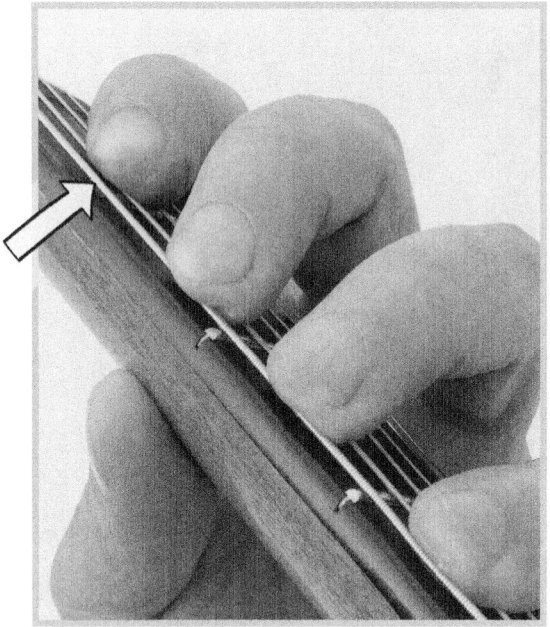

Move 1st finger

2

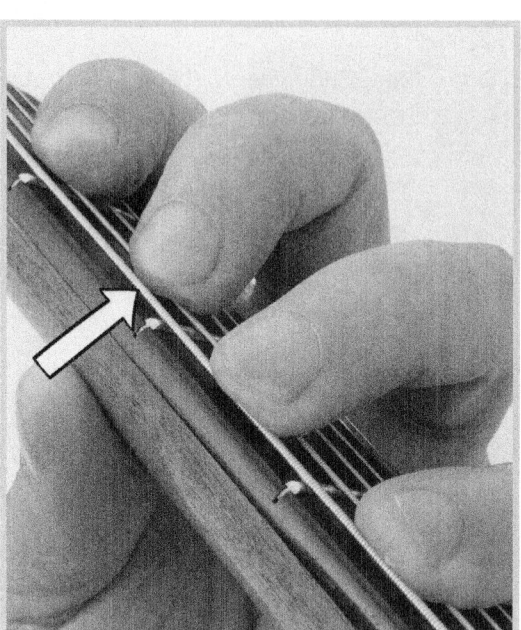

Move 2nd finger

CRAMP

Do you feel cramp during this exercise? Don't worry. It's quite normal. Rest your hand until you feel ready to start again. Once your hand is strong it won't cramp anymore.

This exercise really exposes any weakness in your chord hand and fingers in relation to playing guitar. But it's also the solution.

3

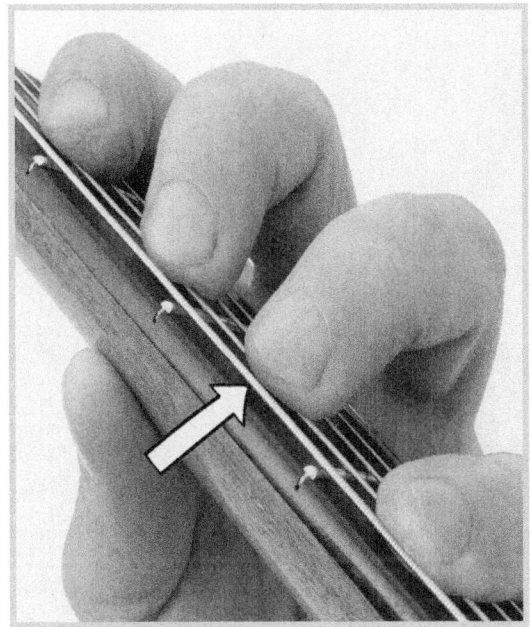

Move 3rd finger

4

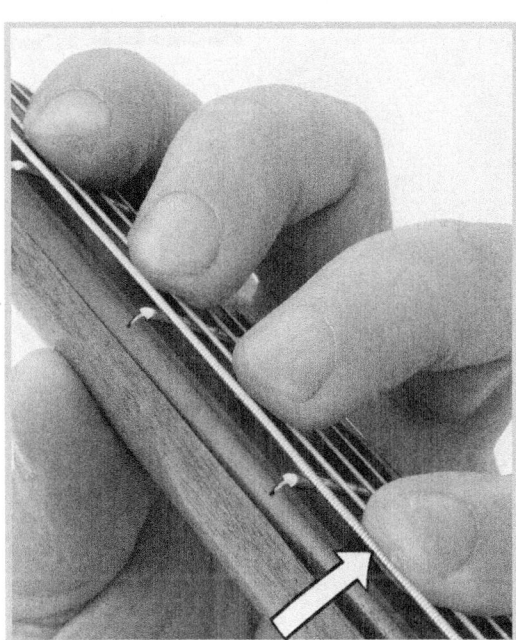

Move 4th finger

- Once you arrive at the finish you can practice back up one finger at a time.

- Start with the 1st finger up one string, then the 2nd finger up one string, then the 3rd and so on.

- Keep going until all four fingers are back on the sixth string. You will find it much easier going back up.

3 EASY CHORD CHANGES

As you saw earlier, it dramatically increases your speed of progress to learn at least two chords at a time.

The real art of your chord hand is not the chords you play. It's what happens between them.

For the next 3 chords your first finger stays in the same position. Am to D7 to Fmaj7. Again, there is no need to move it when changing from chord to chord.

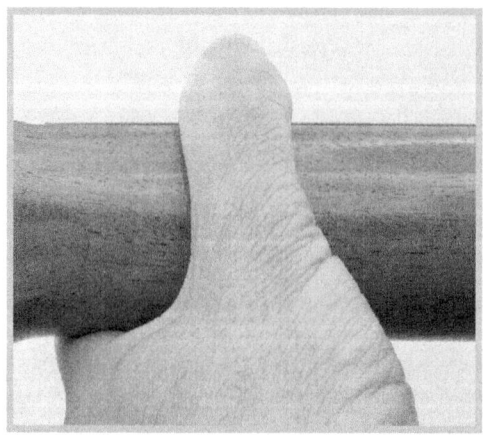

Next 3 chords - **Thumb on Top**

Am

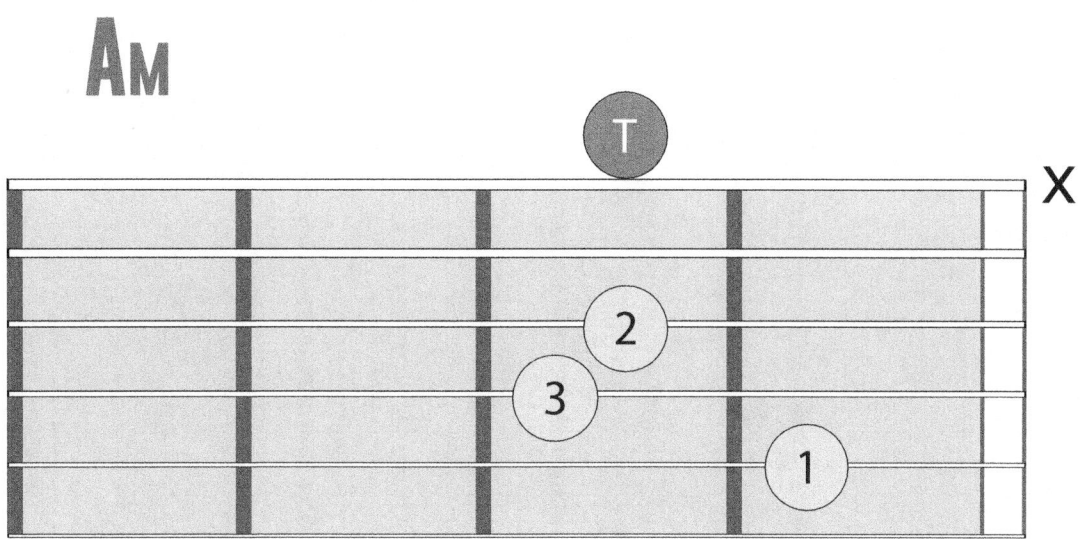

- Thumb touching 6th string
- 1st finger in corner of fret
- Strum 6 strings - Only 5 sound

D7

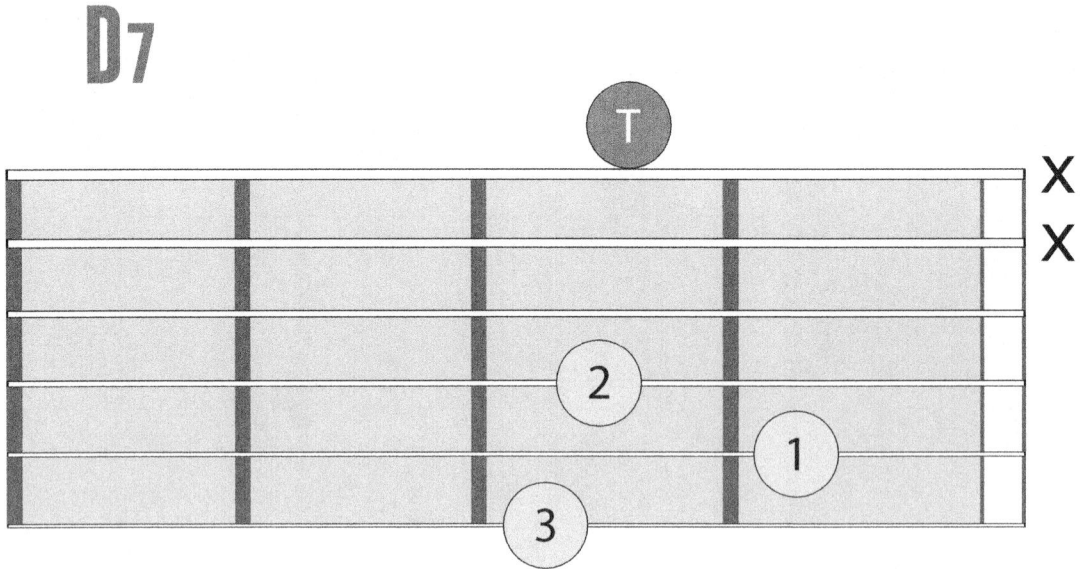

- Thumb touching 6th string
- 1st finger in corner of fret
- Strum bottom 4 strings

Fmaj7

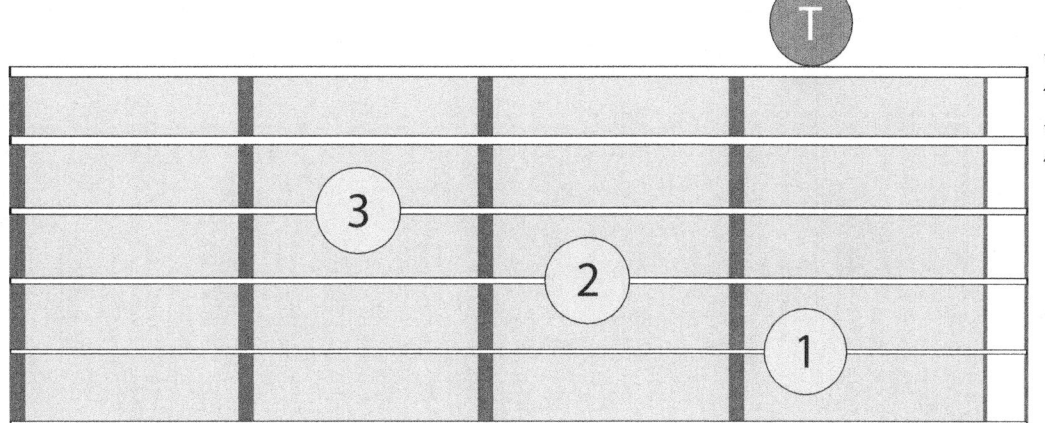

- Thumb touching 6th string
- 1st finger in corner of fret
- Strum bottom 4 strings

56 LEARN & PLAY GUITAR

PLAYING EXERCISE

 **SONG EXAMPLE**
Happy Birthday

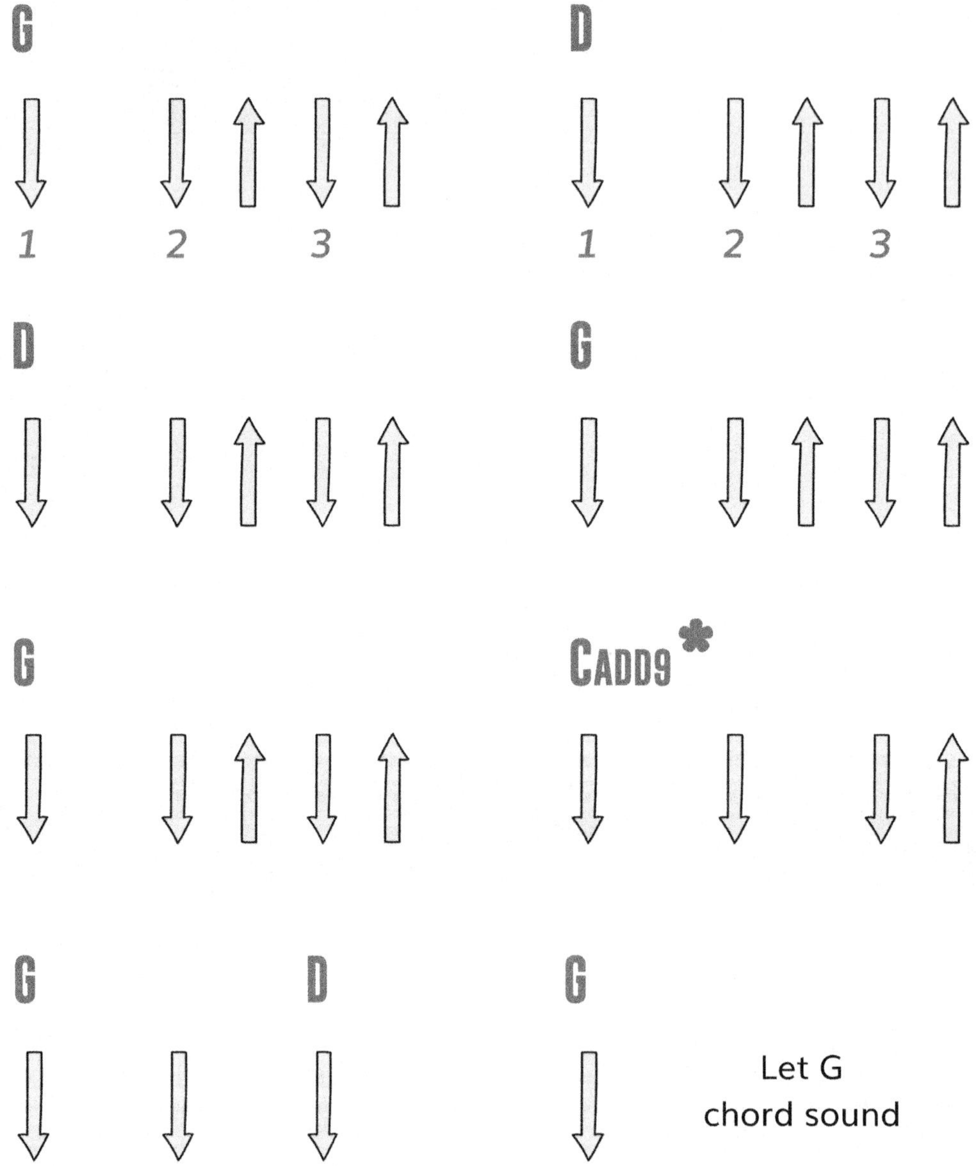

G
↓ ↓ ↑ ↓ ↑
1   2   3

D
↓ ↓ ↑ ↓ ↑
1   2   3

D
↓ ↓ ↑ ↓ ↑

G
↓ ↓ ↑ ↓ ↑

G
↓ ↓ ↑ ↓ ↑

Cadd9 *

↓ ↓ ↓ ↑

G
↓

D
↓

G
↓

G
↓

Let G
chord sound

Keep repeating this chord sequence

PLAYING EXERCISE

SONG EXAMPLE
Holding Back The Years - *Simply Red*

FMAJ7

↓ ↓ ↑ ↑ ↓ ↑

G6

↓ ↓ ↑ ↑ ↓ ↑

FMAJ7

↓ ↓ ↑ ↑ ↓ ↑

G6

↓ ↓ ↑ ↑ ↓ ↑

Keep repeating this chord sequence

HOW TO TIME GUITAR RHYTHMS

1. Can you listen to a slow song that you know well?

2. As it's playing pick up your guitar and mute the strings with your chord hand. Count   1   2   3   4   --   1   2   3   4.

3. If that does not work put on another slow song until you can clearly hear 1   2   3   4   --   1   2   3   4.

4. Start softly strumming the strings up and down until you are on time with the song.

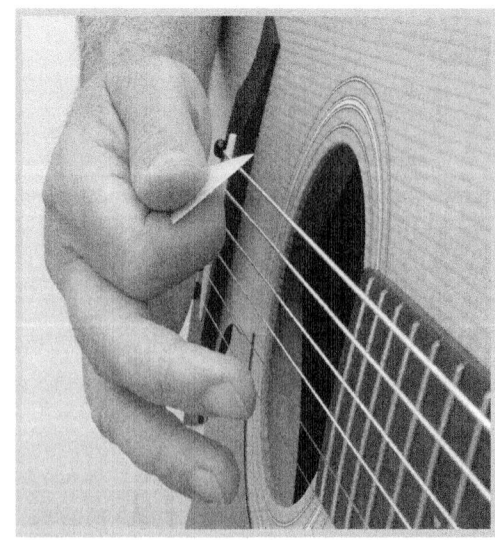

Very Important - A good hold

Your chord hand keeps the strings muted while you are doing this. It's so much easier to strum when you don't have the added pressure of playing chords at the same time.

Eventually you should be able to find a rhythm to suit any song you want to play. It may not be exactly as recorded but the timing will be right. Also your own style will be starting to develop.

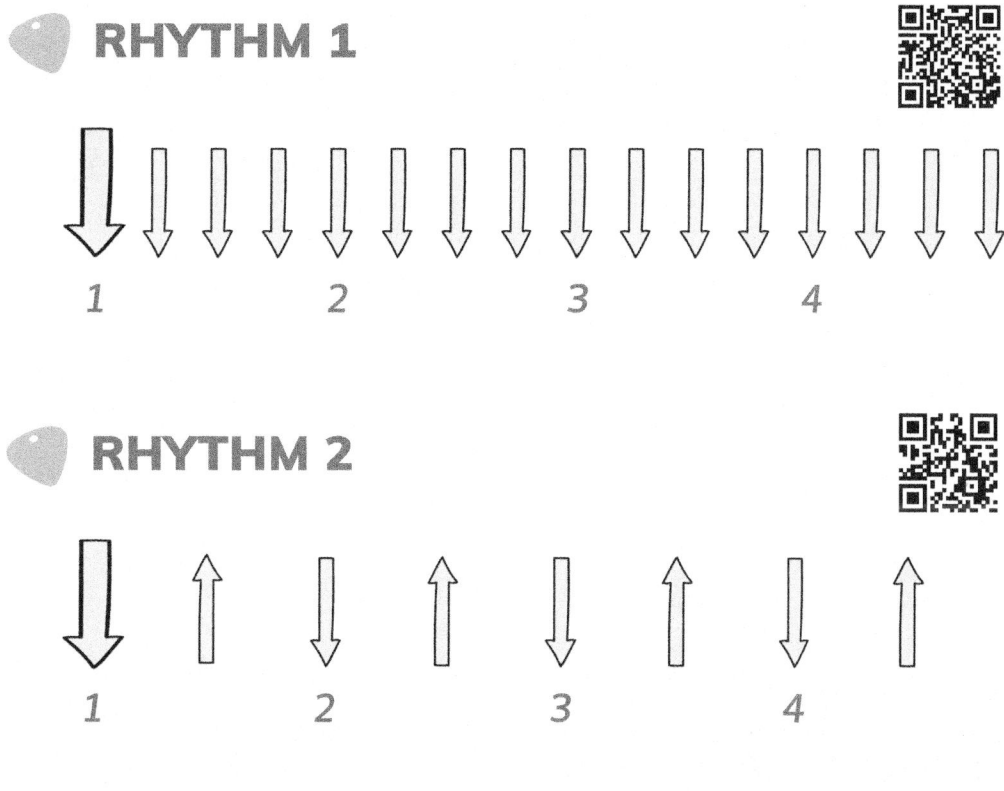

Em7

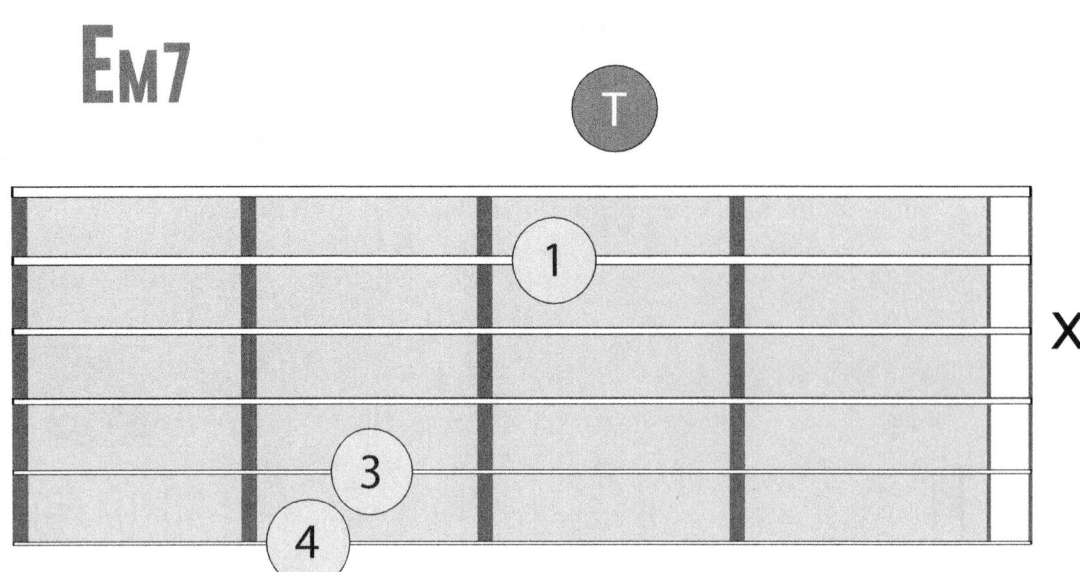

- Thumb not touching 6th string
- 4th string muted by inside of 1st finger
- Strum 6 strings - Only 5 sound

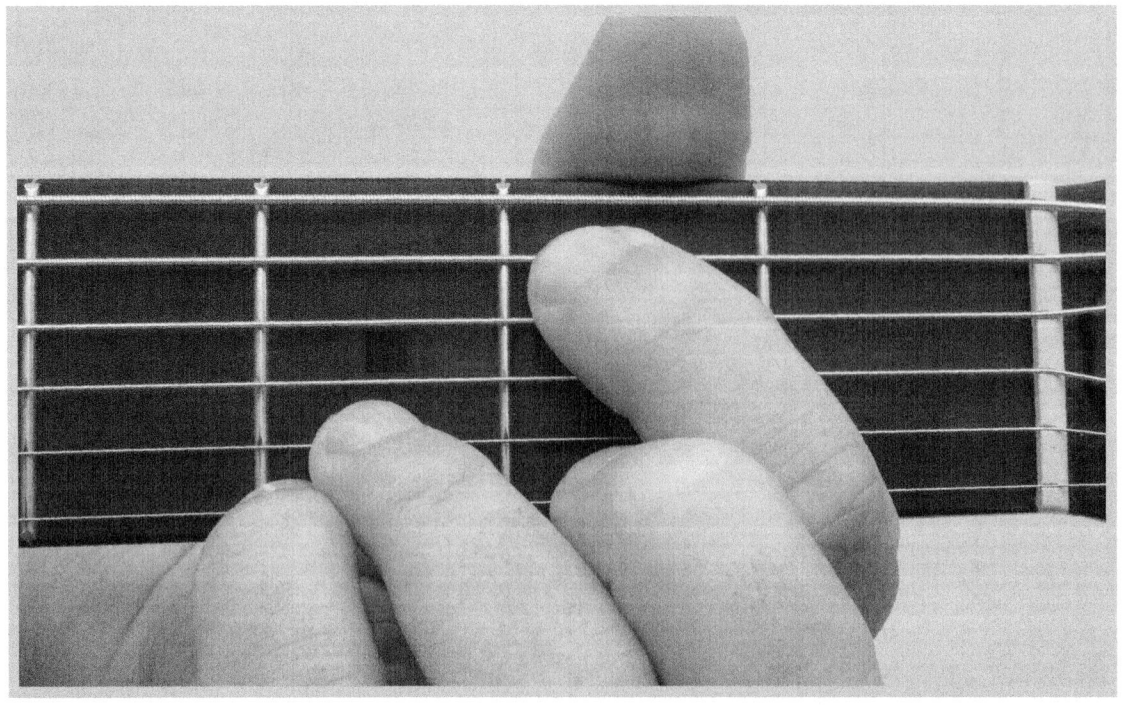

Dsus2

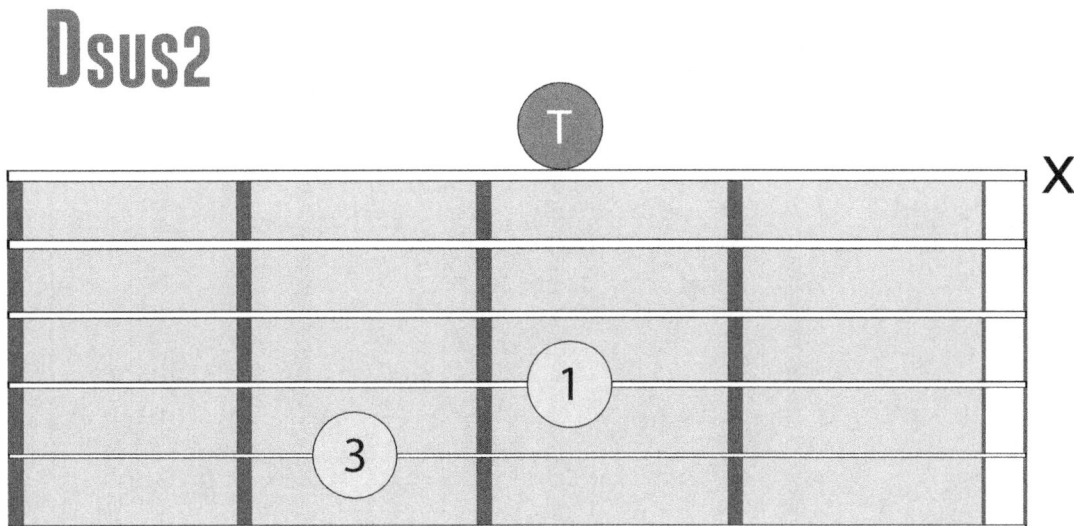

- Thumb touching 6th string
- 3rd finger in middle of fret
- Strum 6 strings - Only 5 sound

C

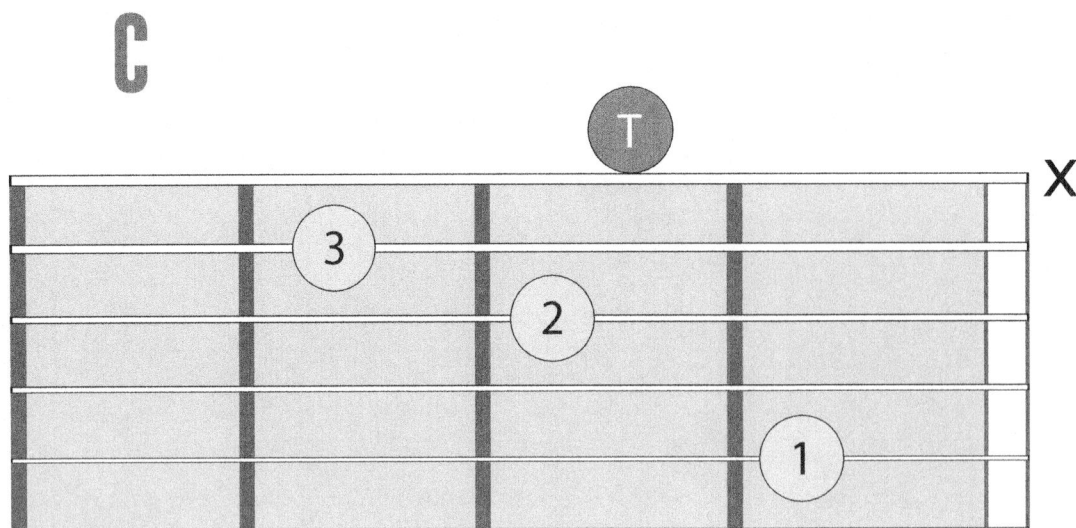

- Thumb touching 6th string
- 1st finger in corner of fret
- Strum 6 strings - Only 5 sound

Asus2

- Thumb touching 6th string
- 2nd finger in corner of fret
- Strum 6 strings - Only 5 sound

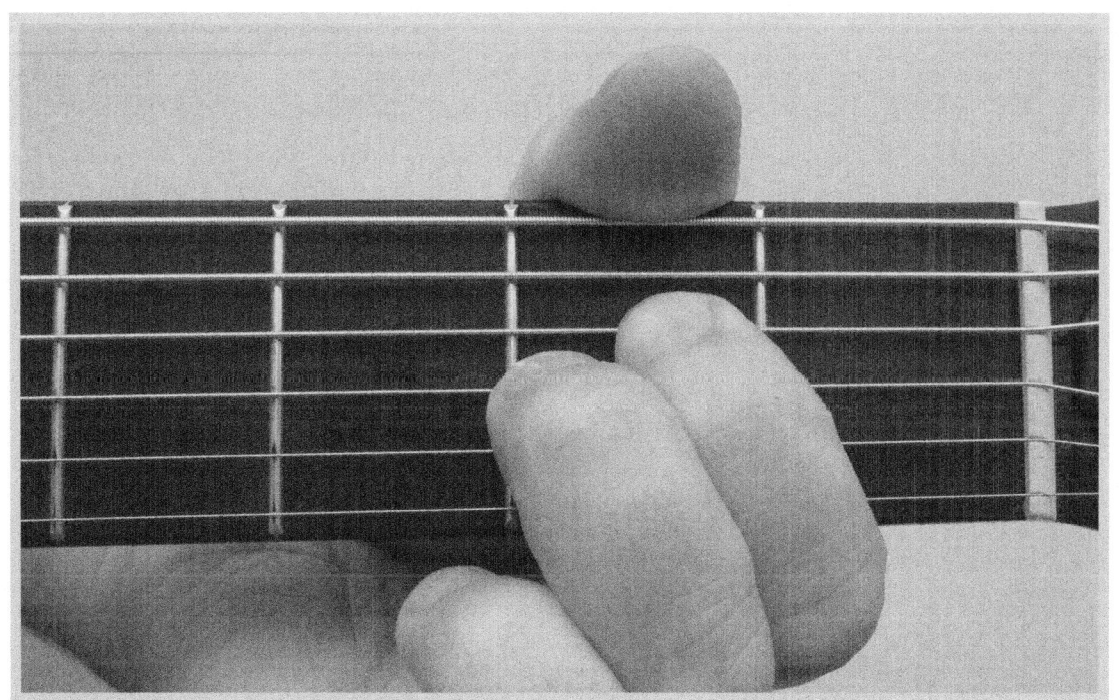

PLAYING EXERCISE

SONG EXAMPLE
Wicked Game - Chris Isaak

CAPO ON 2ND FRET

Am

G

D

D

Keep repeating this chord sequence

PLAYING EXERCISE

SONG EXAMPLE
Mad World - *Tears For Fears*

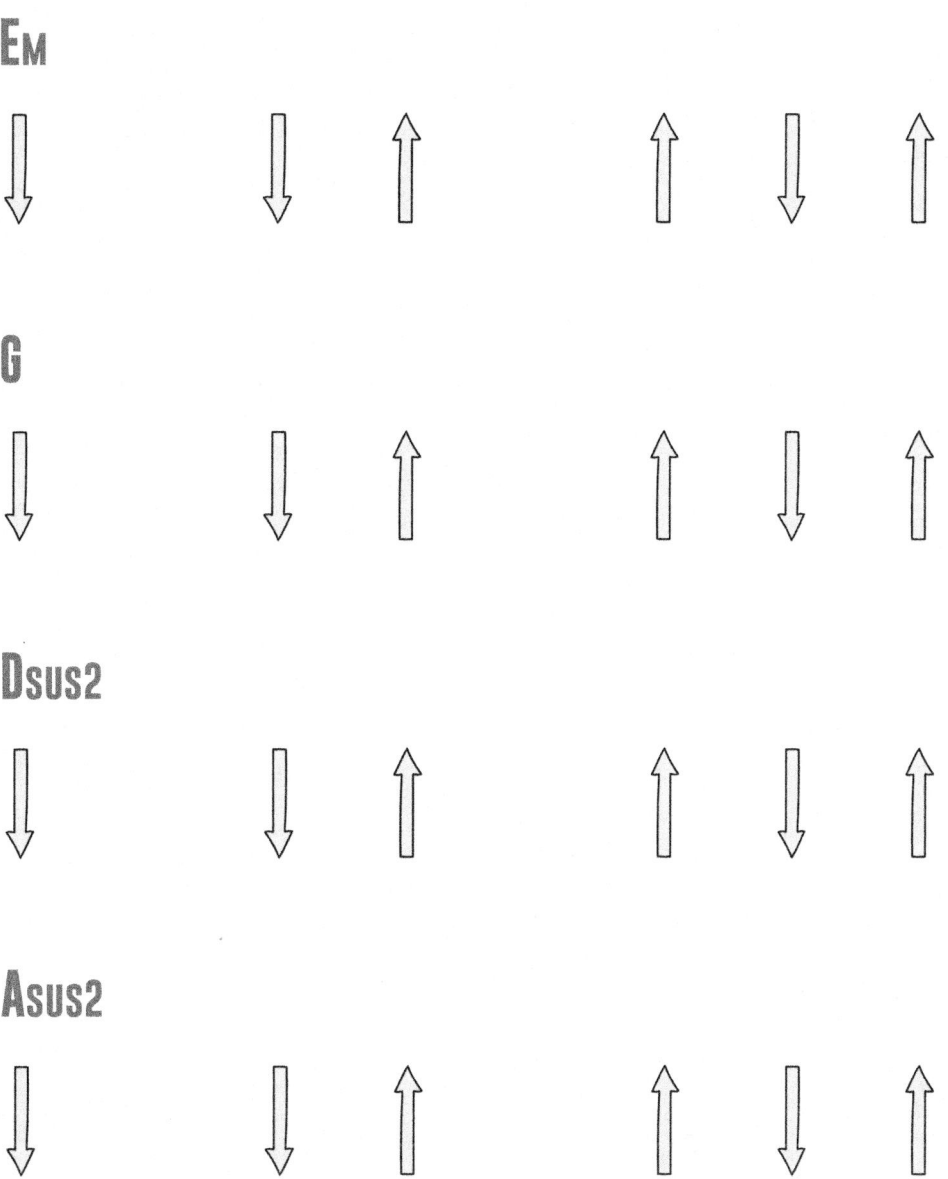

Keep repeating this chord sequence

PLAYING EXERCISE

SONG EXAMPLE
What's Up - 4 Non Blondes

CAPO ON 2ND FRET

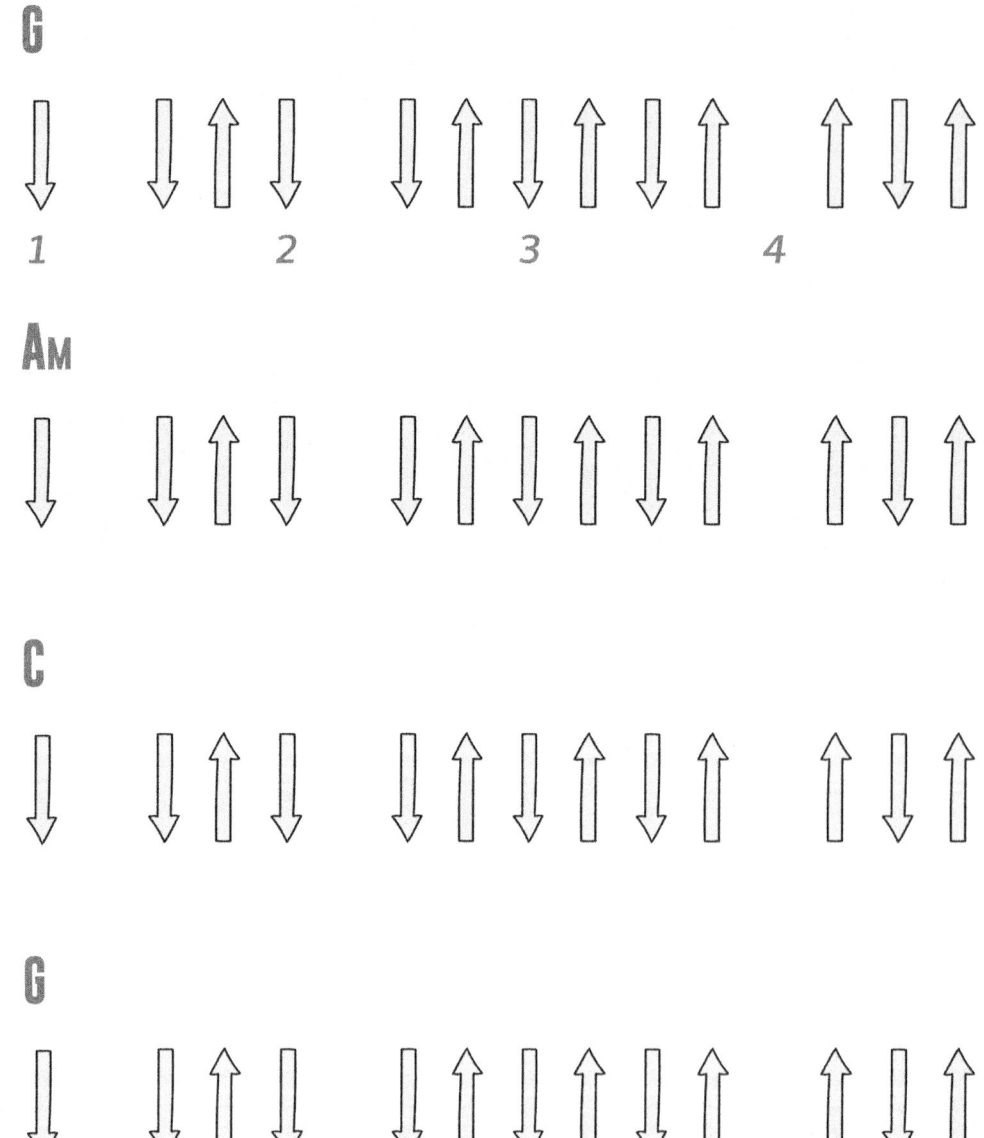

Keep repeating this chord sequence

PLAYING EXERCISE

SONG EXAMPLE
Viva la Vida
Coldplay

CAPO ON 1ST FRET

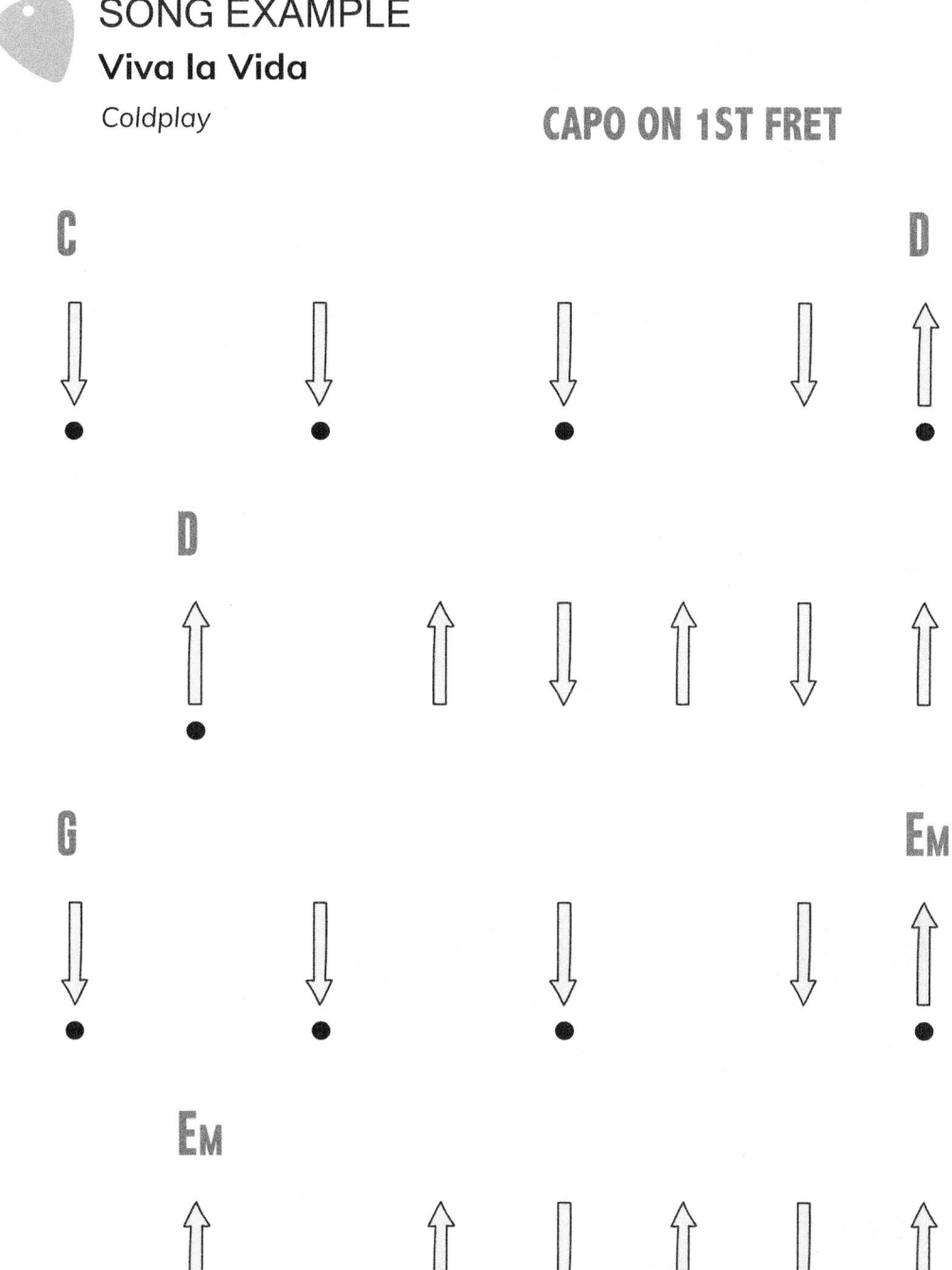

Keep repeating this chord sequence

Asus4

- Thumb touching 6th string
- 3rd finger in middle of fret
- Strum 6 strings - Only 5 sound

G/F#

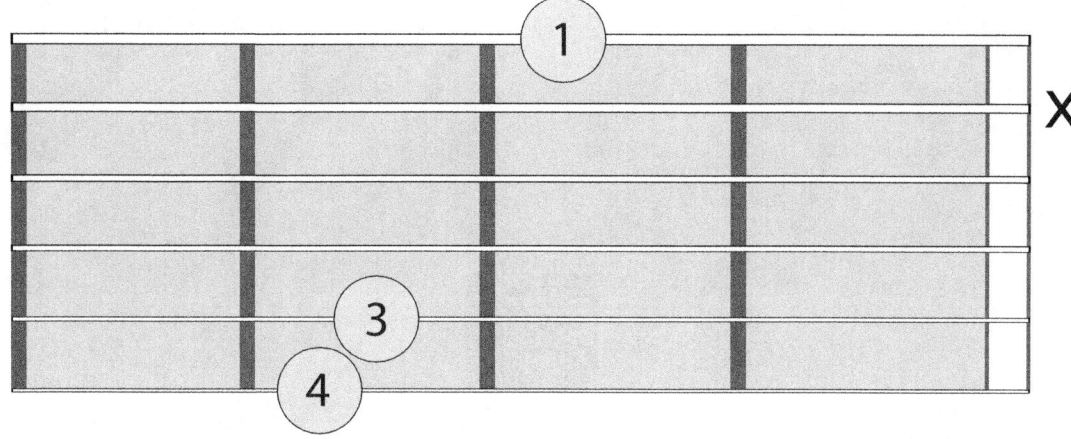

- Thumb may or may not touch 6th string
- 5th string muted by inside of 1st finger
- Strum 6 strings - Only 5 sound

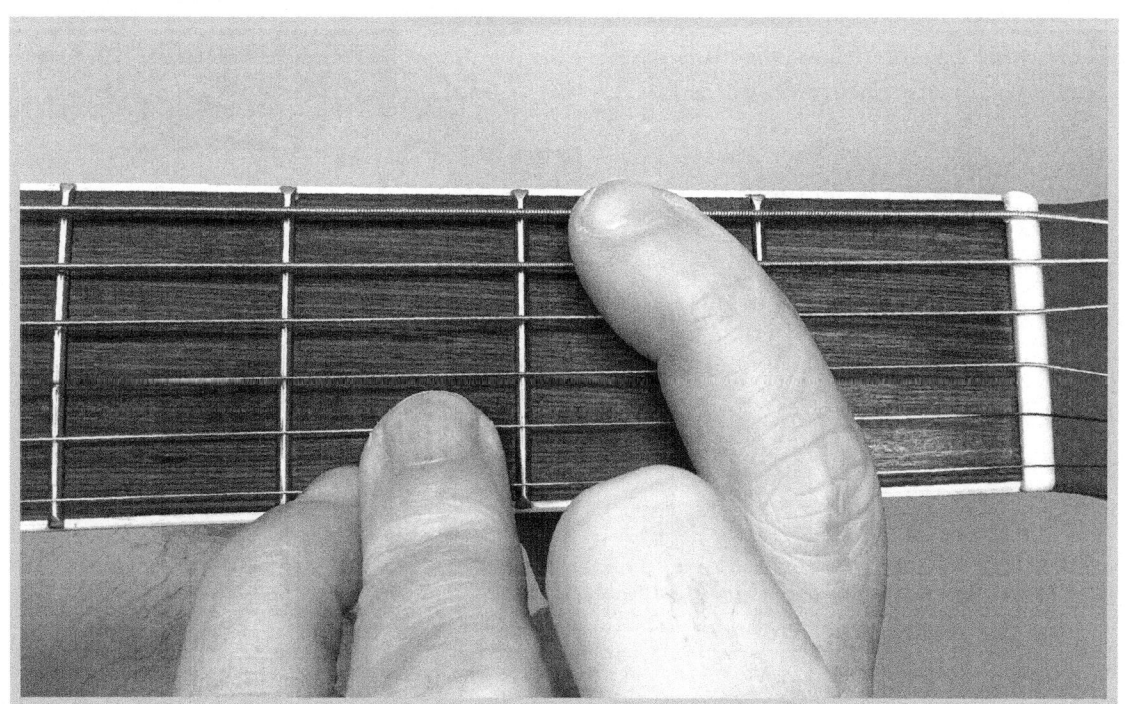

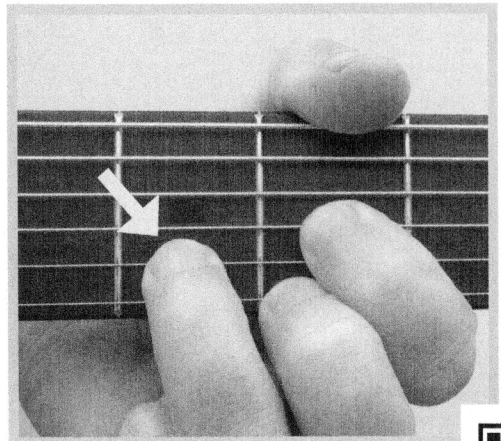
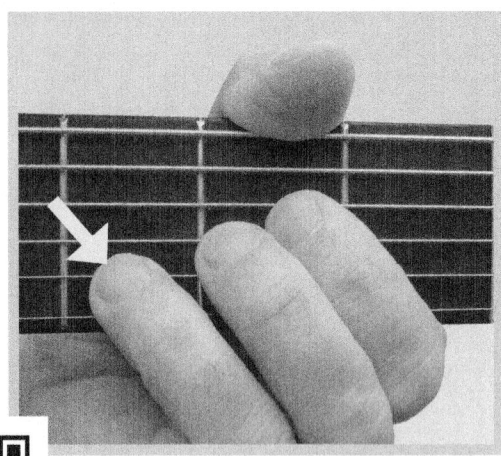

🎸 MORE EASY CHORD CHANGES

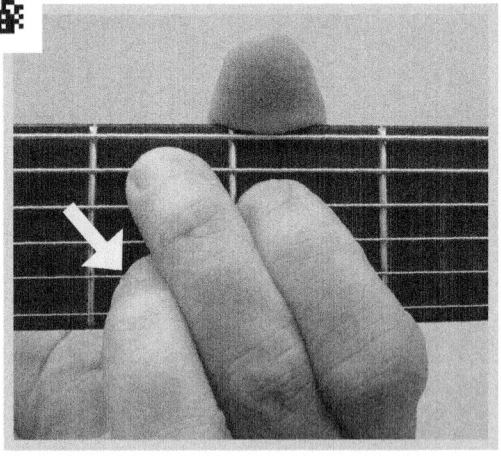

You can play tens of thousands of songs on guitar without moving your thumb, 3rd finger, or triangle. This keeps your fingers close to the strings and your chord changing becomes much faster.

If you look closely at all these chords you'll see:

1 The 3rd finger is in the same place for all of them

2 The 3rd finger stays constantly pressed into the string

3 The Guitar Triangle

4 The 1st and 2nd fingers do most of the changing. Your hand stays almost still.

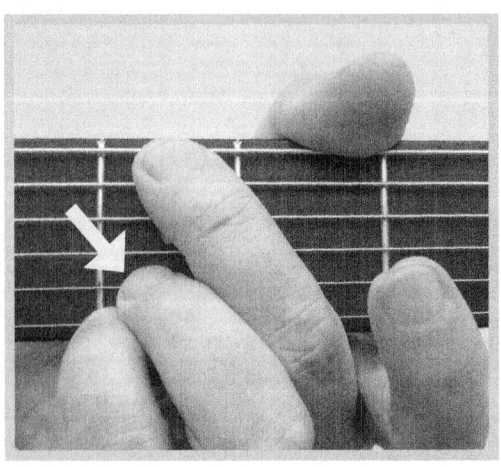

PLAYING EXERCISE

 **SONG EXAMPLE**
Free Falling - Tom Petty

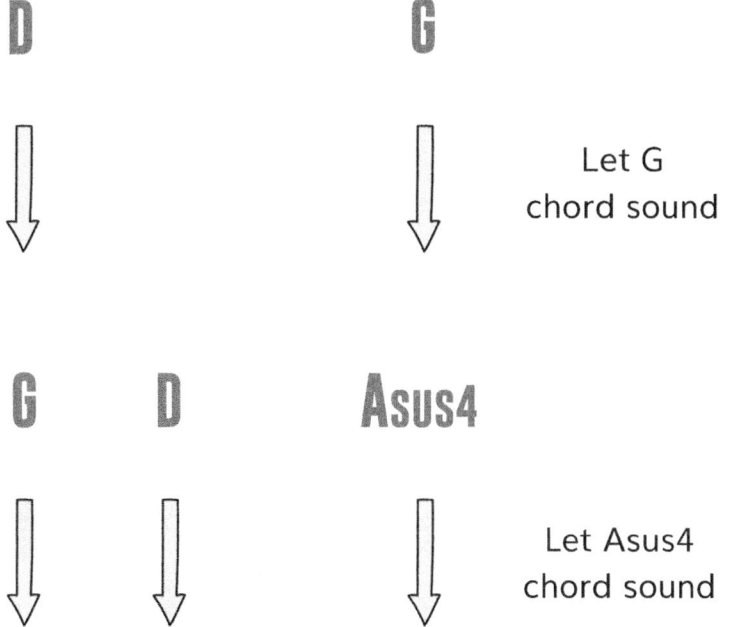

Keep repeating this chord sequence

 ## PLAYING TIP

When changing, don't move your

1 3rd finger

2 Triangle

PLAYING EXERCISE

SONG EXAMPLE

I'm Yours - Jason Mraz

CAPO ON 4TH FRET

G

↓   ↓ ↑ ↓ ↑ ↓ ↑   ↓   ↓ ↑ ↓ ↑ ↓ ↑

D

↓   ↓ ↑ ↓ ↑ ↓ ↑   ↓   ↓ ↑ ↓ ↑ ↓ ↑

Em7

↓   ↓ ↑ ↓ ↑ ↓ ↑   ↓   ↓ ↑ ↓ ↑ ↓ ↑

Cadd9

↓   ↓ ↑ ↓ ↑ ↓ ↑   ↓   ↓ ↑ ↓ ↑ ↓ ↑

Keep repeating this chord sequence

PLAYING EXERCISE

SONG EXAMPLE
Riptide - Vance Joy

CAPO ON 1ST FRET

Am
↓ ↓ ↑ ↓ ↑

G
↓ ↓ ↑ ↓ ↑

C
↓ ↓ ↑ ↓ ↑

C
↓ ↓ ↑ ↓ ↑

Keep repeating this chord sequence

PLAYING EXERCISE

SONG EXAMPLE
Chasing Cars - *Snow Patrol*

CAPO ON 2ND FRET

G

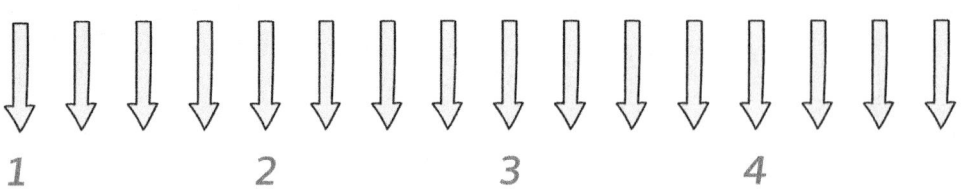

1   2   3   4

G/F#

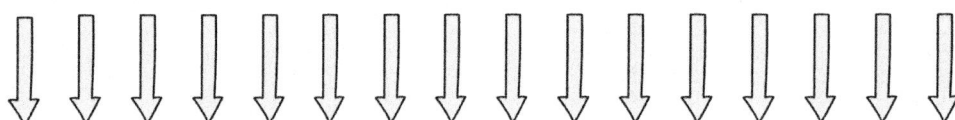

Cadd9

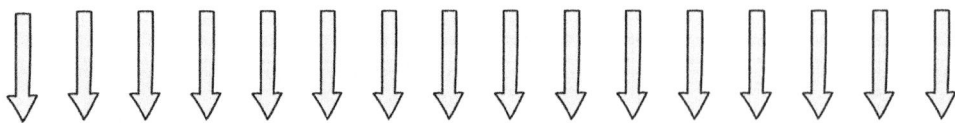

G

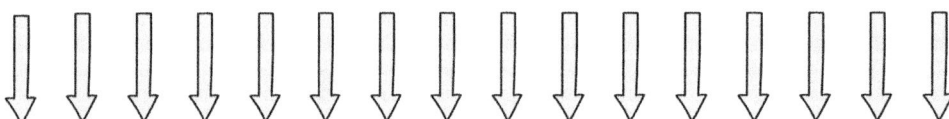

Keep repeating this chord sequence

PLAYING EXERCISE

SONG EXAMPLE
Yellow - *Coldplay*

CAPO ON 4TH FRET

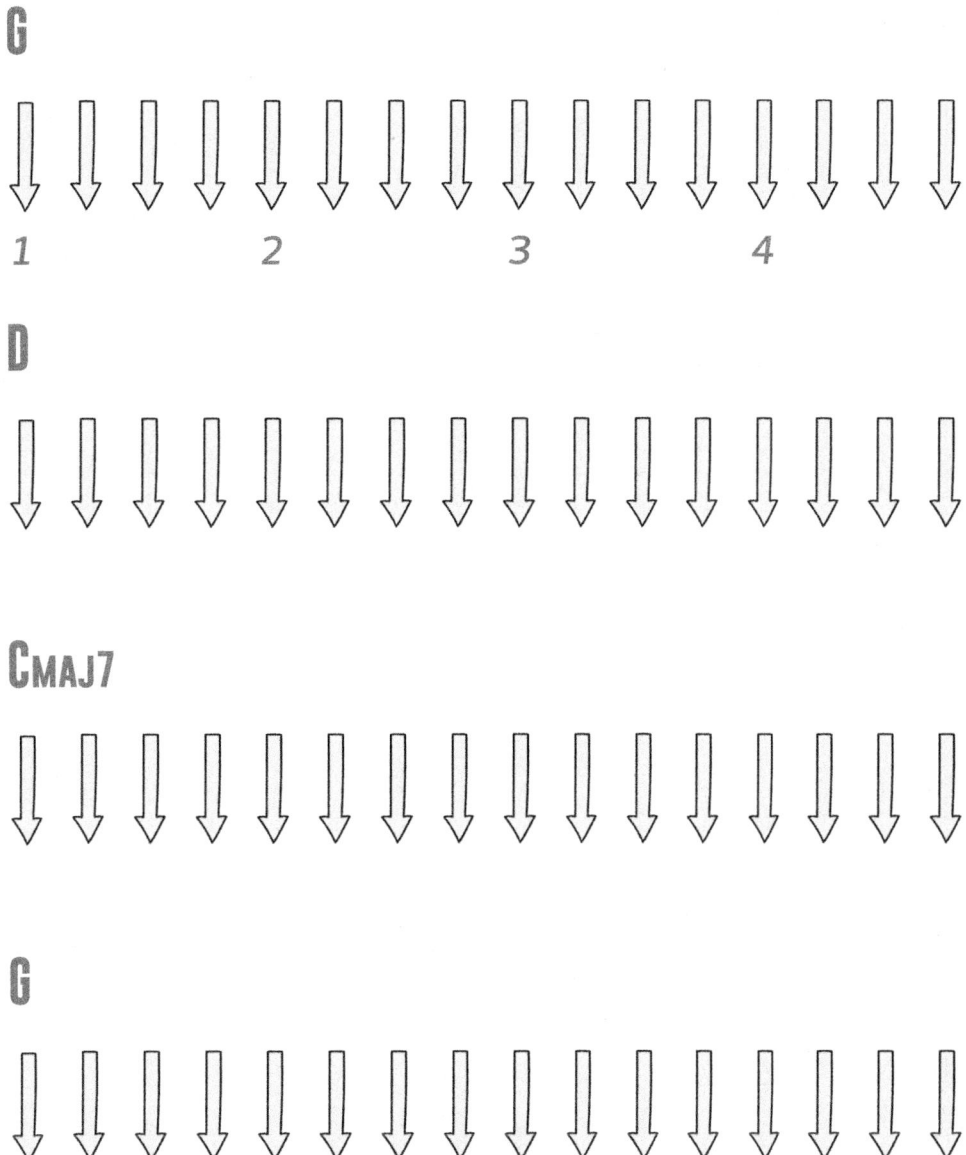

Keep repeating this chord sequence

SONG EXAMPLE
Don't Worry, Be Happy
Bobby McFerrin

PLAYING EXERCISE

CAPO ON 4TH FRET

G

G

Am

Am

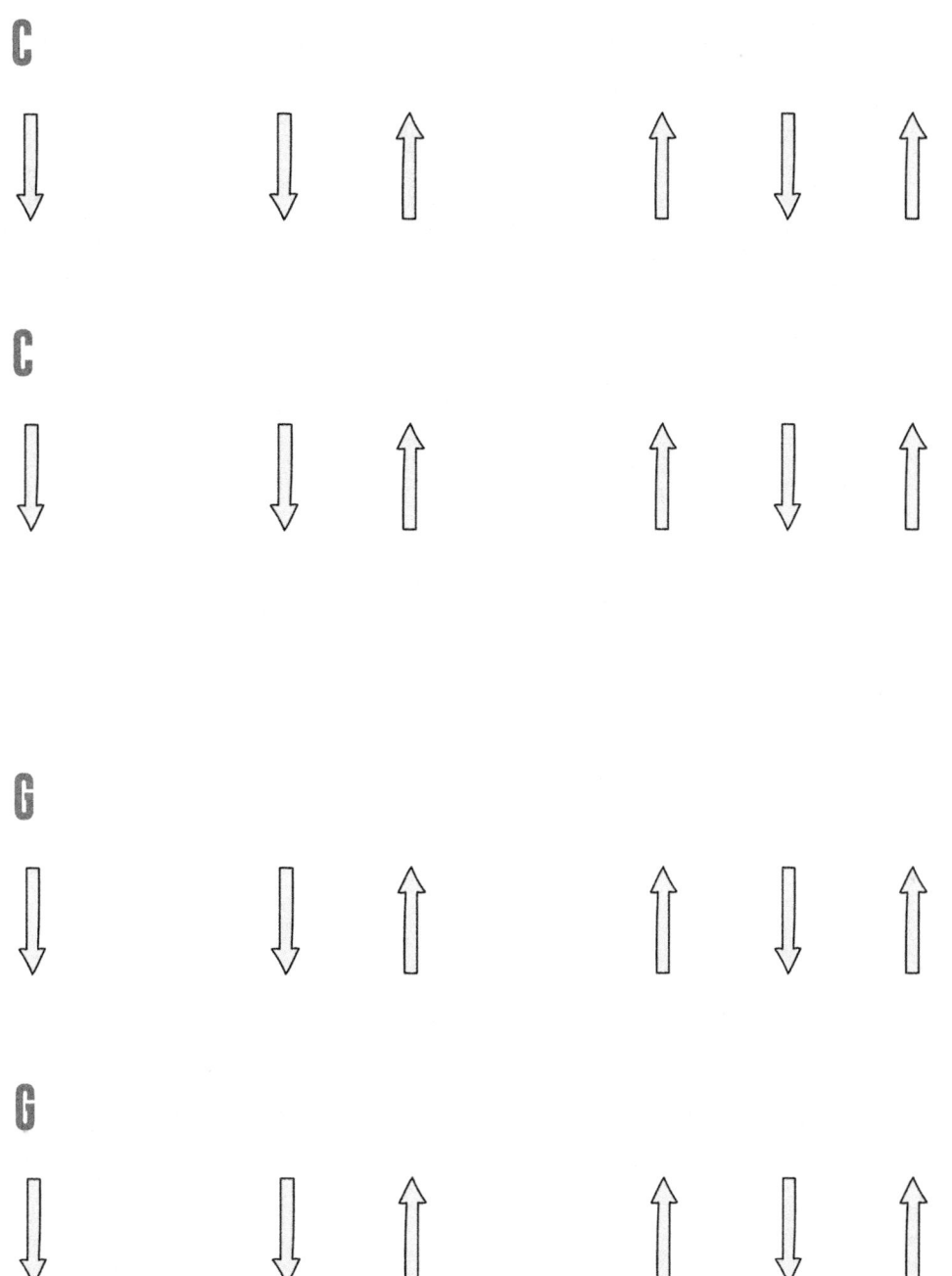

Keep repeating this chord sequence

PLAYING EXERCISE

 **SONG EXAMPLE**
Leaving On A Jetplane - *John Denver*

G

⬇ ⬇ ⬆ ⬆ ⬇ ⬆

Cadd9 *

⬇ ⬇ ⬆ ⬆ ⬇ ⬆

G

⬇ ⬇ ⬆ ⬆ ⬇ ⬆

Cadd9 *

⬇ ⬇ ⬆ ⬆ ⬇ ⬆

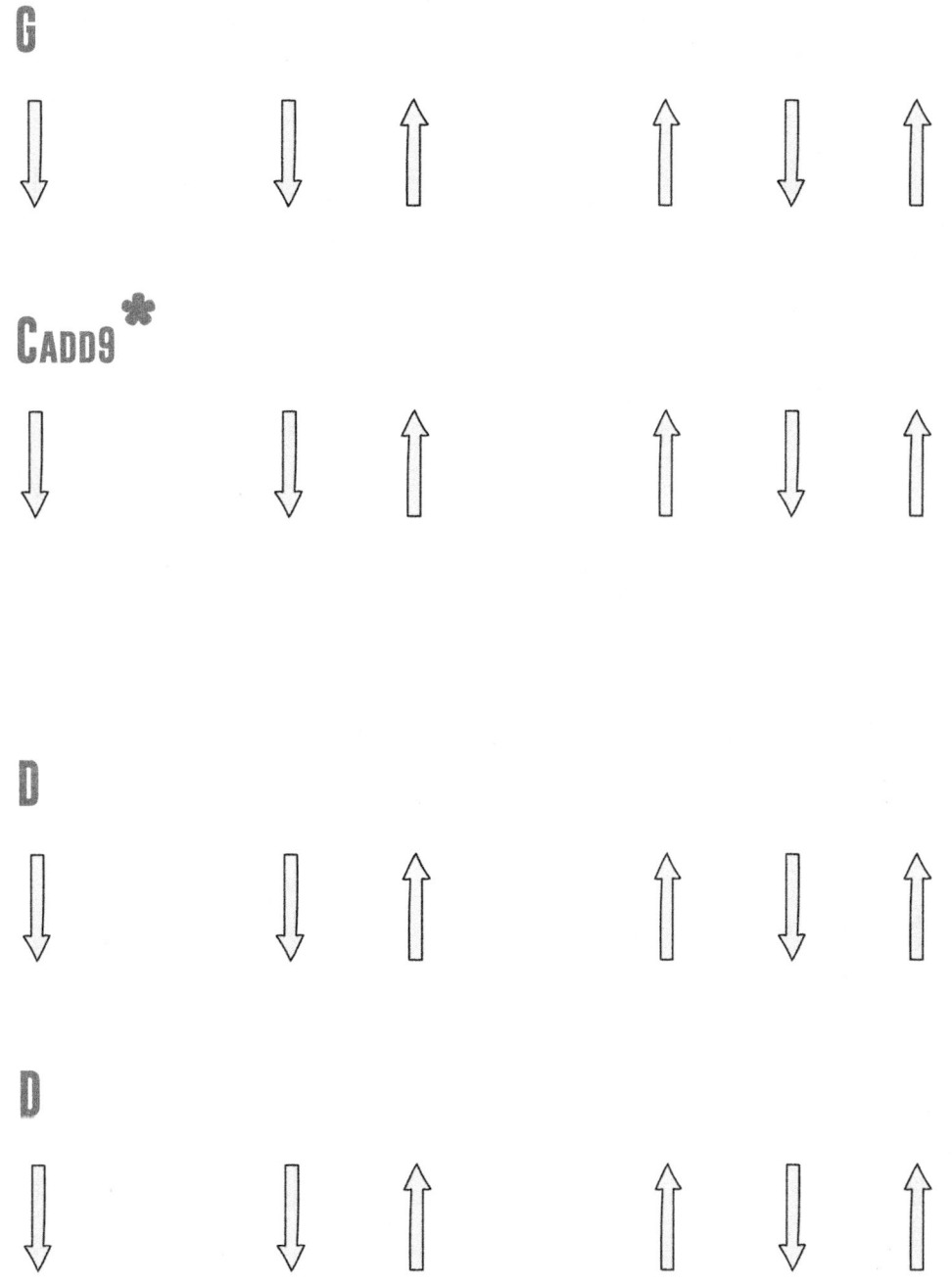

Keep repeating this chord sequence

PLAYING EXERCISE

 SONG EXAMPLE
Stand By Me - Ben E King

CAPO ON 2ND FRET

G

 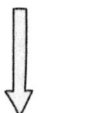   

G

Em

 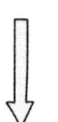    

Em

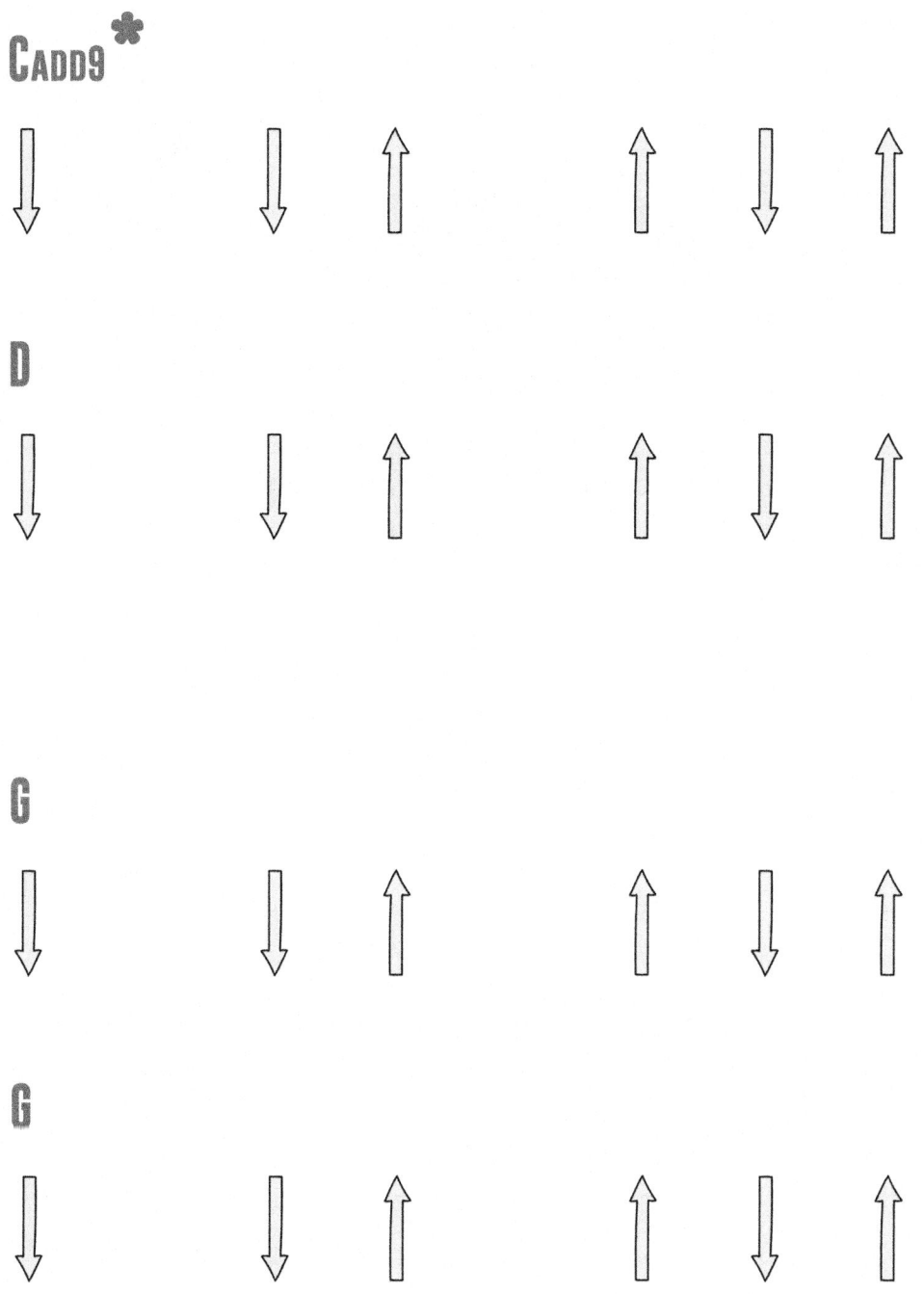

Keep repeating this chord sequence

Guitar tablature is very easy to learn. The six horizontal lines represent the six strings on the guitar. The numbers are the frets to play. 0 = Open String. 2 = 2nd Fret.

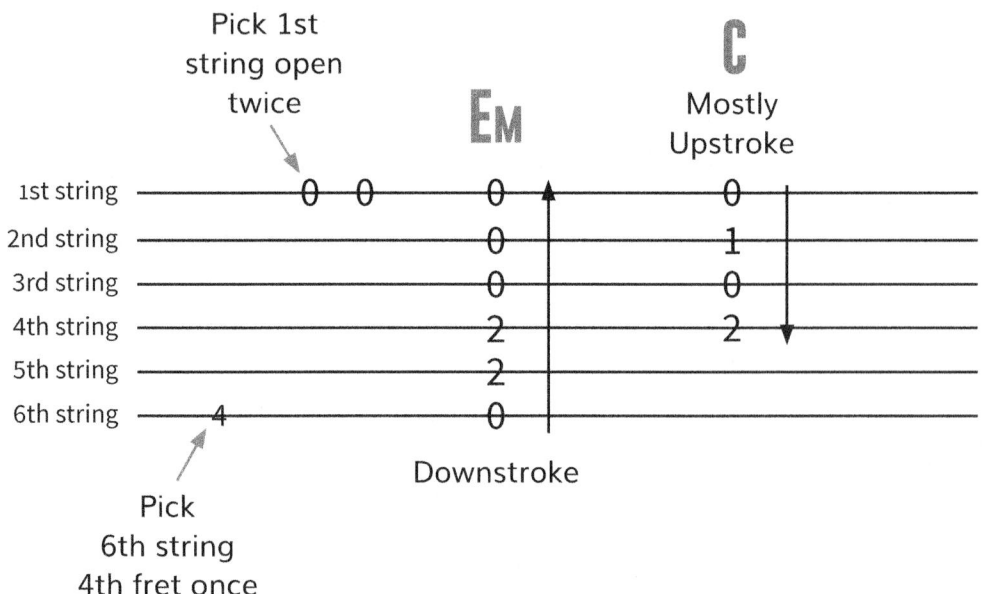

PLAYING EXERCISE

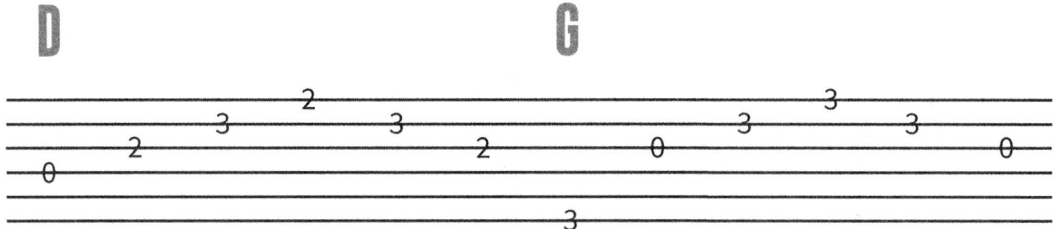

If the numbers are written one after another, you pick the strings one at a time (after you have fingered the chord). If the numbers are written on top of each other, you play all the strings at once (strumming).

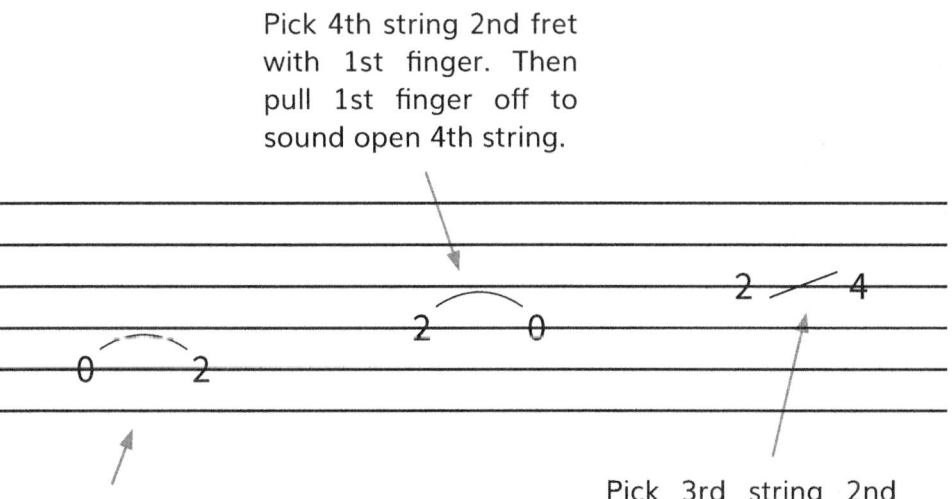

Pick 4th string 2nd fret with 1st finger. Then pull 1st finger off to sound open 4th string.

Pick 5th string open. Then hammer on to 5th string 2nd fret with 2nd finger.

Pick 3rd string 2nd fret. Then slide finger to 3rd string 4th fret.

HOW TO PLAY FINGERSTYLE GUITAR

Competent guitarists play by feel and without looking at their picking hand. They do this by playing from a reference point.

Many have the heel pad of their hand lightly resting on the bridge pins (pictured right).

Others have the 3rd or 4th finger on the guitar (Next page).

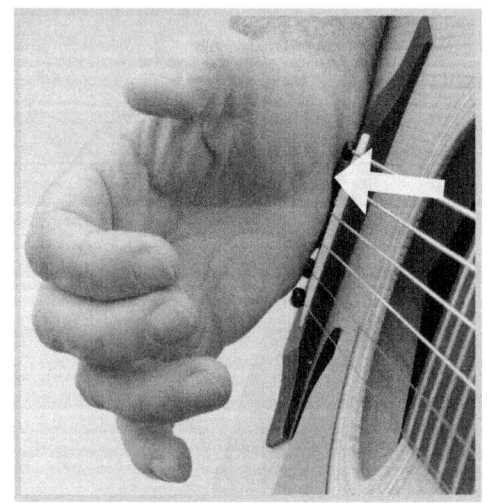

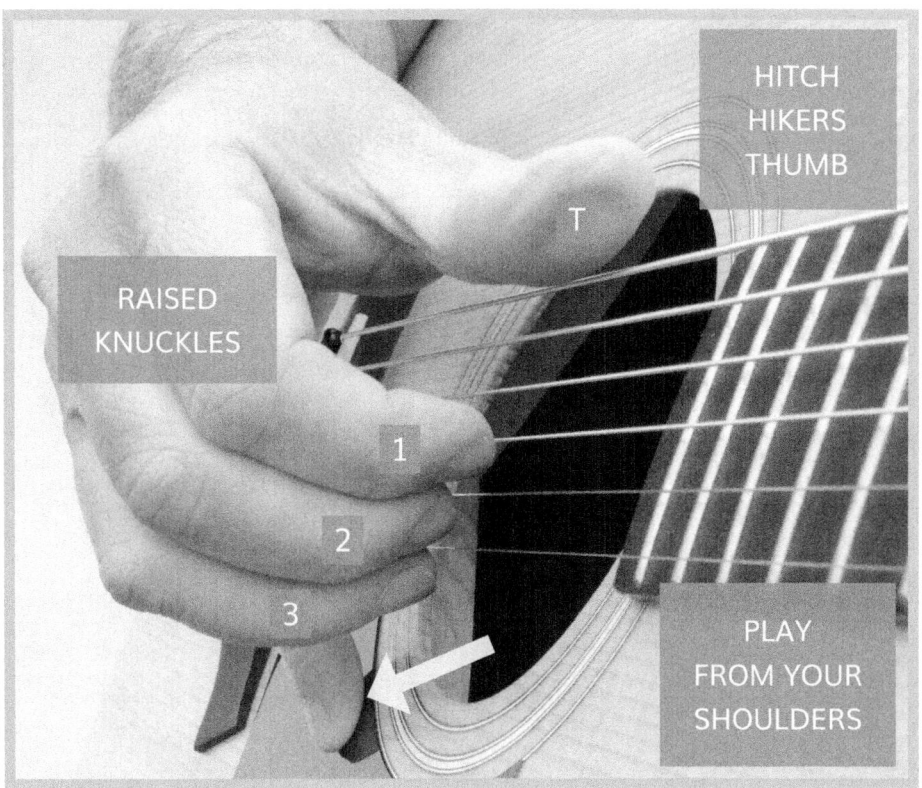

PLAYING TIPS

1. Visualize a ball in your hand
2. Thumb picks down
3. Fingers pick up
4. Thumb picks a little louder than fingers

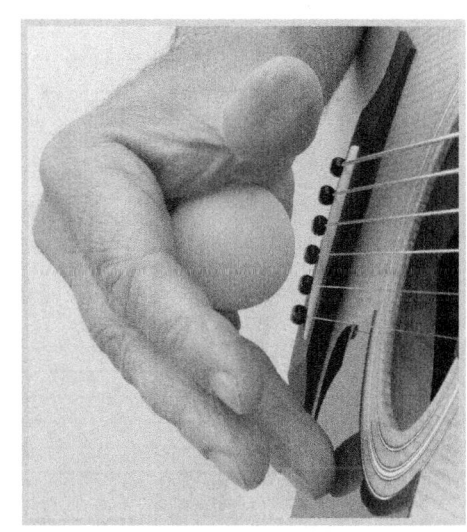

6 POPULAR FINGERSTYLES

G

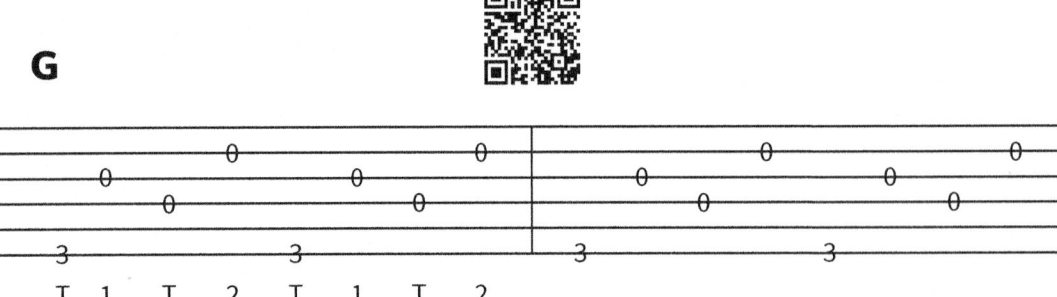

T 1 T 2 T 1 T 2

D

T 1 T 2 T 1 T 2

C

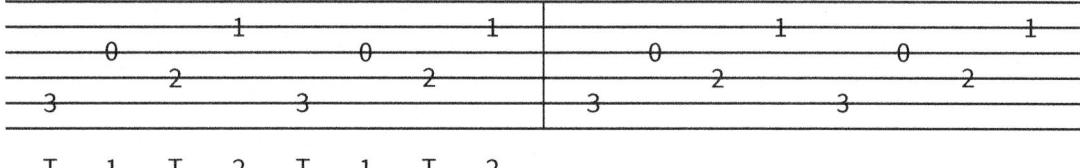

Asus2

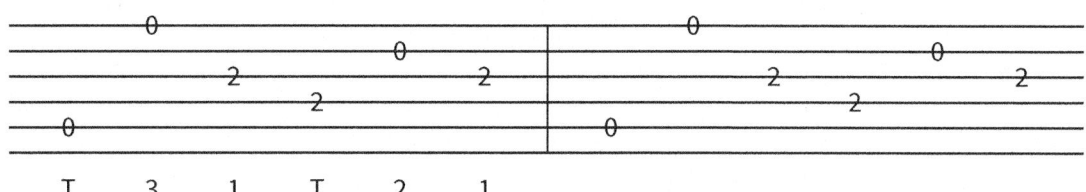

Cmaj7

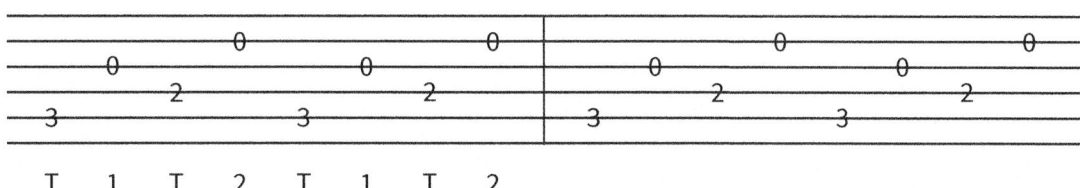

Am

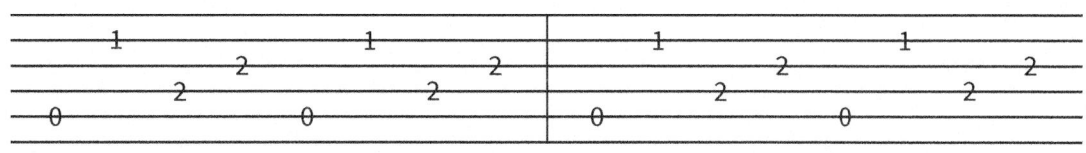

SONG EXAMPLE
ROMANZA

Fingerstyle

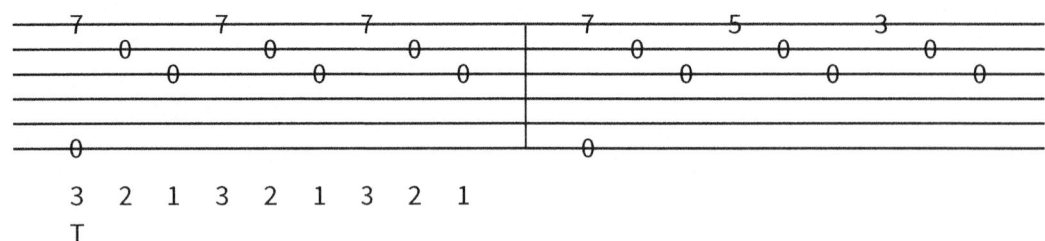

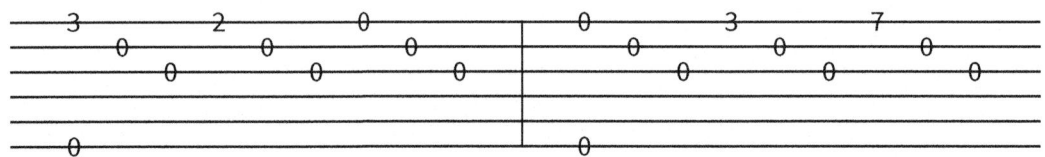

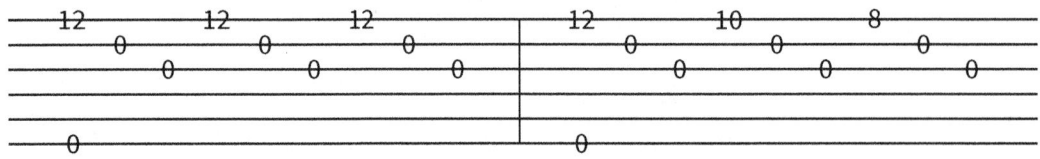

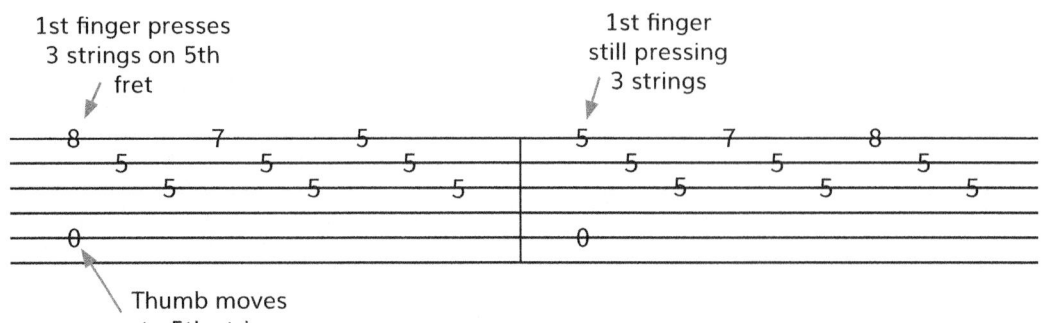

LEARN & PLAY GUITAR

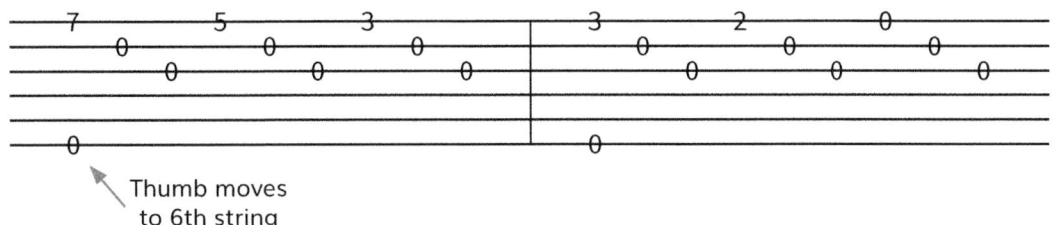

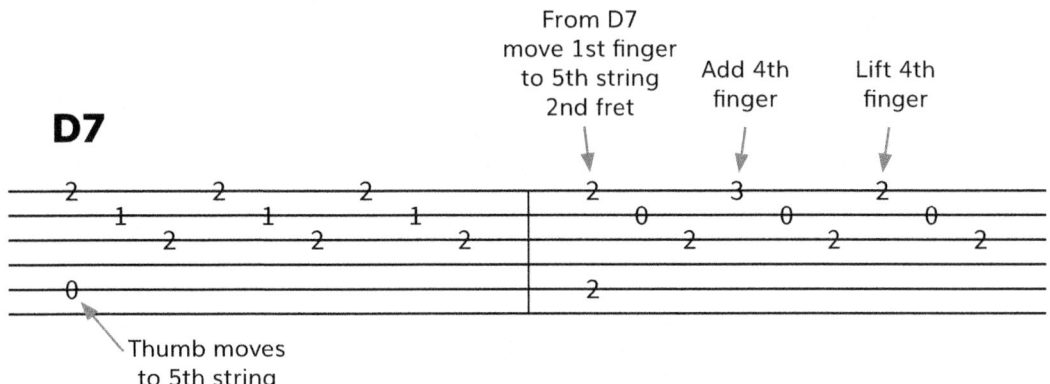

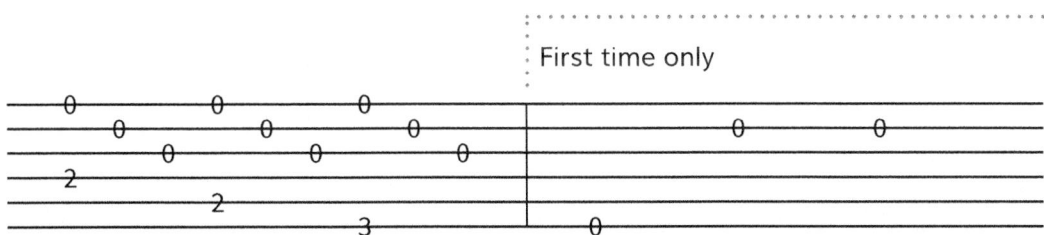

NOW GO BACK TO START

E

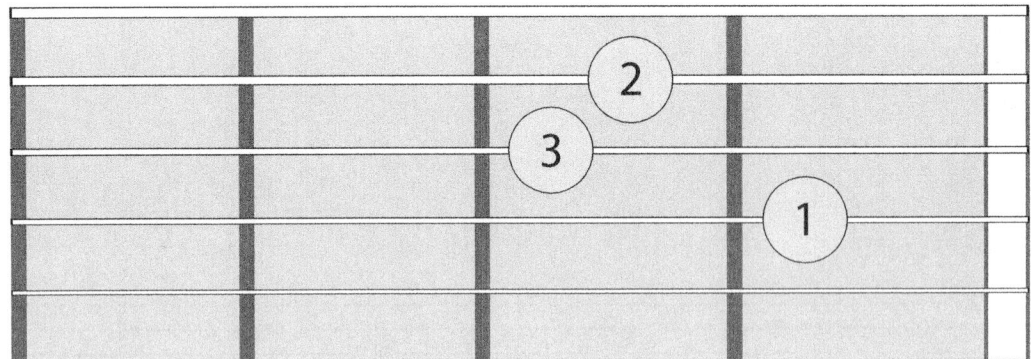

- Thumb not touching 6th string
- 1st finger in corner of fret
- All 6 strings sound

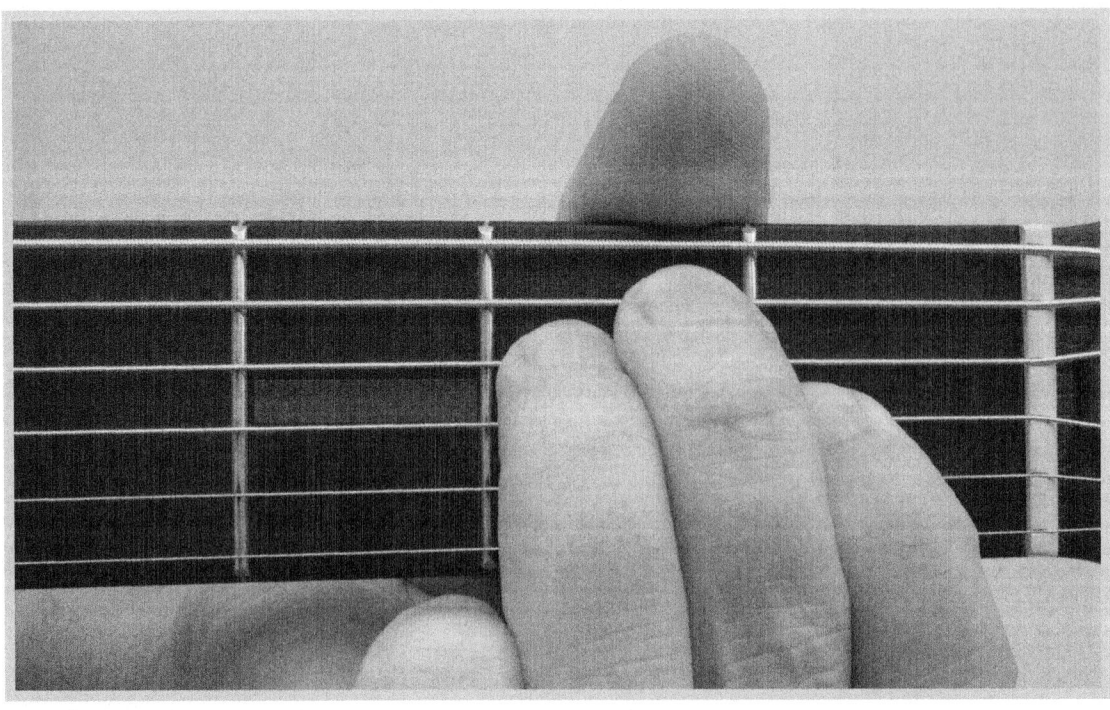

B7

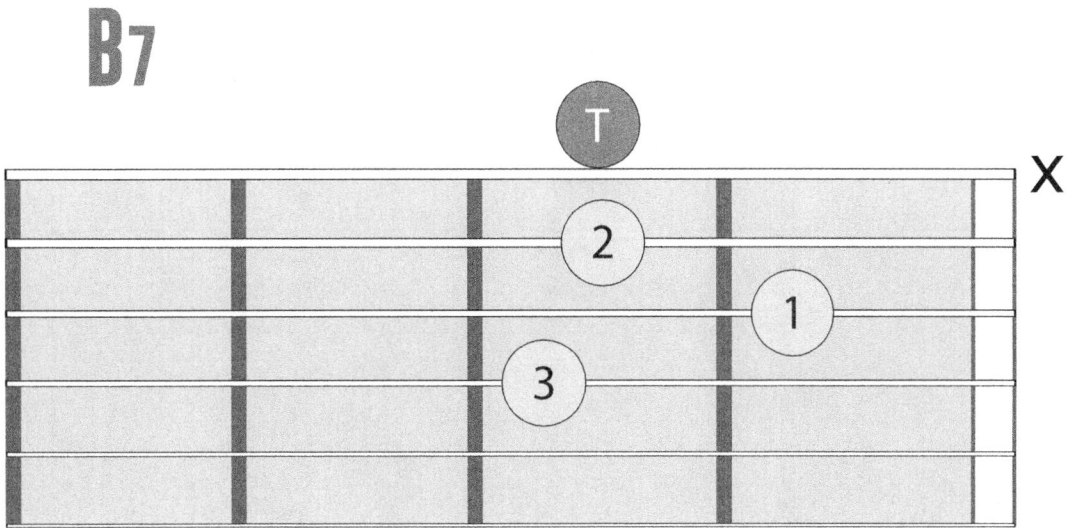

- Thumb touching 6th string
- 1st finger in corner of fret
- Strum 6 strings - Only 5 sound

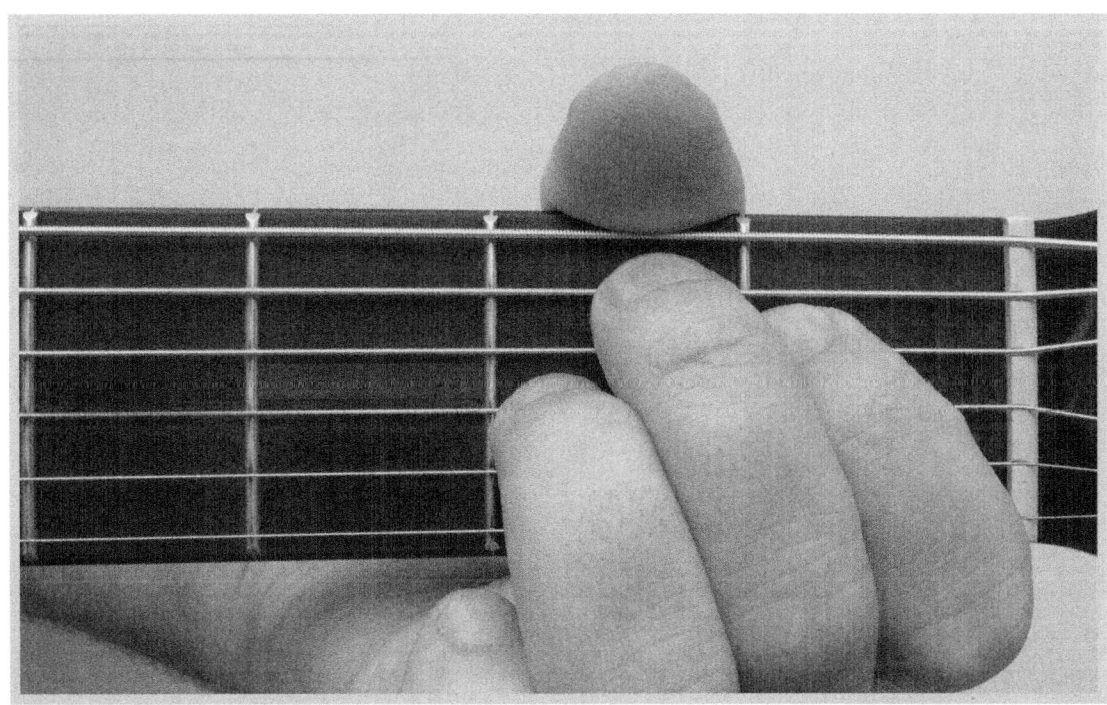

LEARN & PLAY GUITAR

A

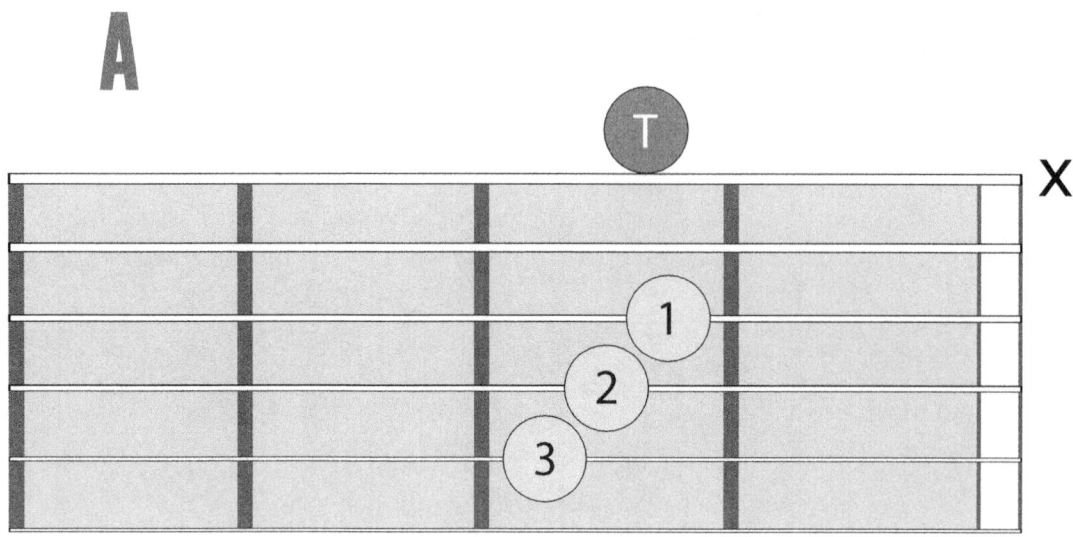

- Thumb touches 6th string
- Squeeze 3 fingers together
- Strum 6 strings - Only 5 sound

PLAYING EXERCISE

SONG EXAMPLE
Dance The Night Away - The Mavericks

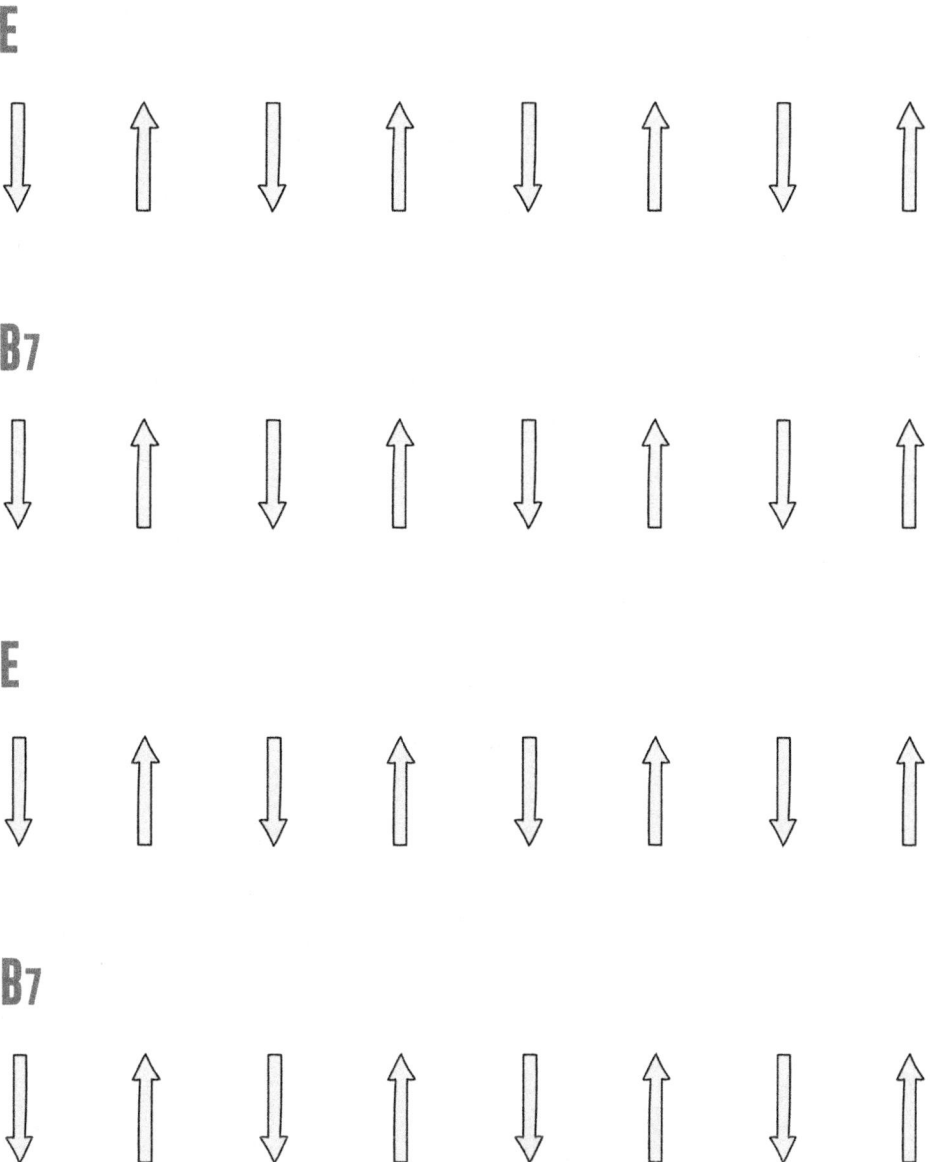

Keep repeating this chord sequence

PLAYING EXERCISE

 SONG EXAMPLE
Peaceful Easy Feeling - *The Eagles*

E

 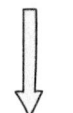   

Asus2

E

 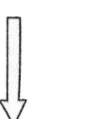   

Asus2

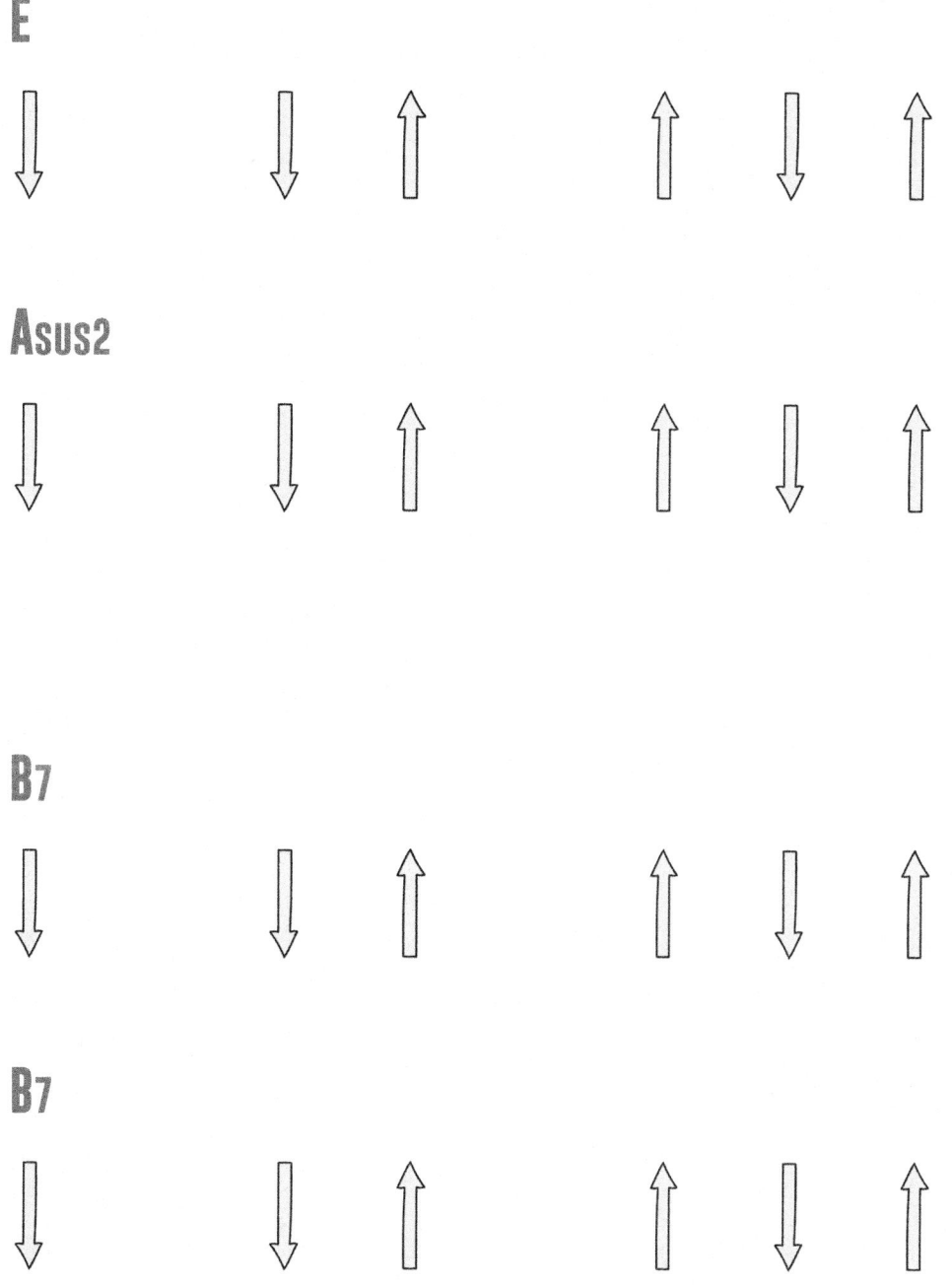

Keep repeating this chord sequence

PLAYING EXERCISE

SONG EXAMPLE
Sweet Home Alabama - *Lynyrd Skynyrd*

D

↓   ↓   ↓ ↑   ↓ ↑

Cadd9

↓   ↓   ↓ ↑   ↓ ↑

G

↓   ↓   ↓ ↑   ↓ ↑

G

↓   ↓   ↓ ↑   ↓ ↑

Keep repeating this chord sequence

PLAYING EXERCISE

SONG EXAMPLE
Time Of Your Life - *Green Day*

G
↓ ↓ ↑ ↑ ↓ ↑

G
↓ ↓ ↑ ↑ ↓ ↑

Cadd9
↓ ↓ ↑ ↑ ↓ ↑

D
↓ ↓ ↑ ↑ ↓ ↑

Keep repeating this chord sequence

Am7

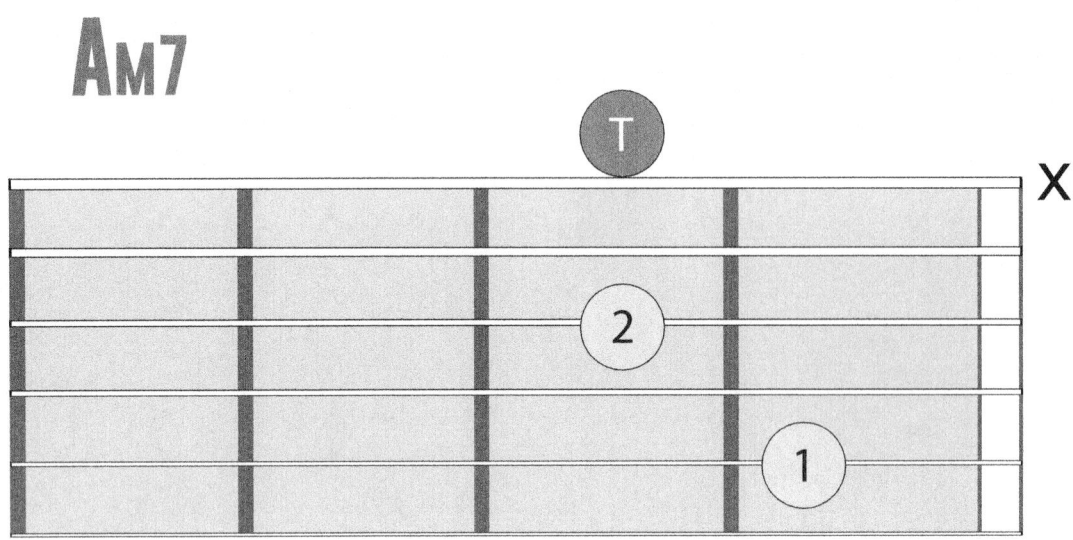

- Thumb touching 6th string
- 1st finger in corner of fret
- Strum 6 strings - Only 5 sound

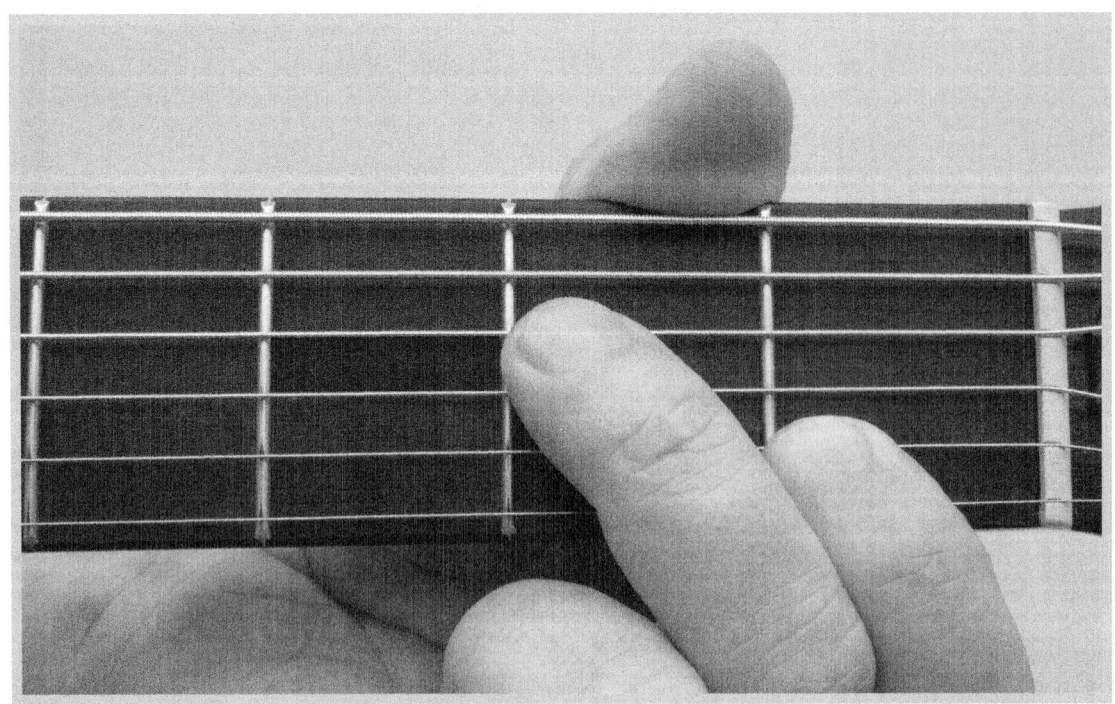

Am7

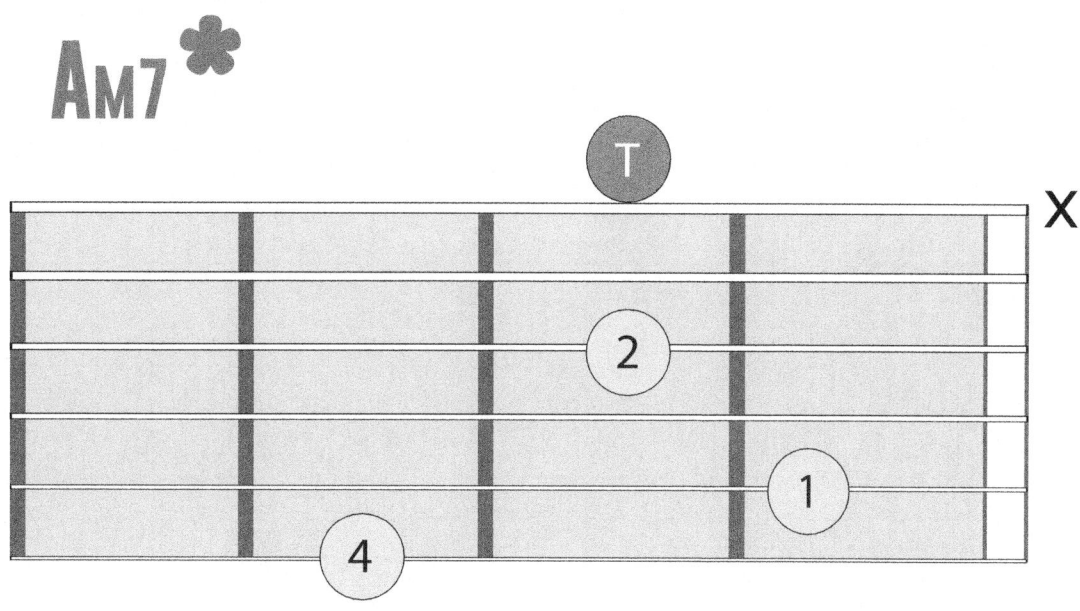

- Thumb touching 6th string
- 1st finger in corner of fret
- Strum 6 strings - Only 5 sound

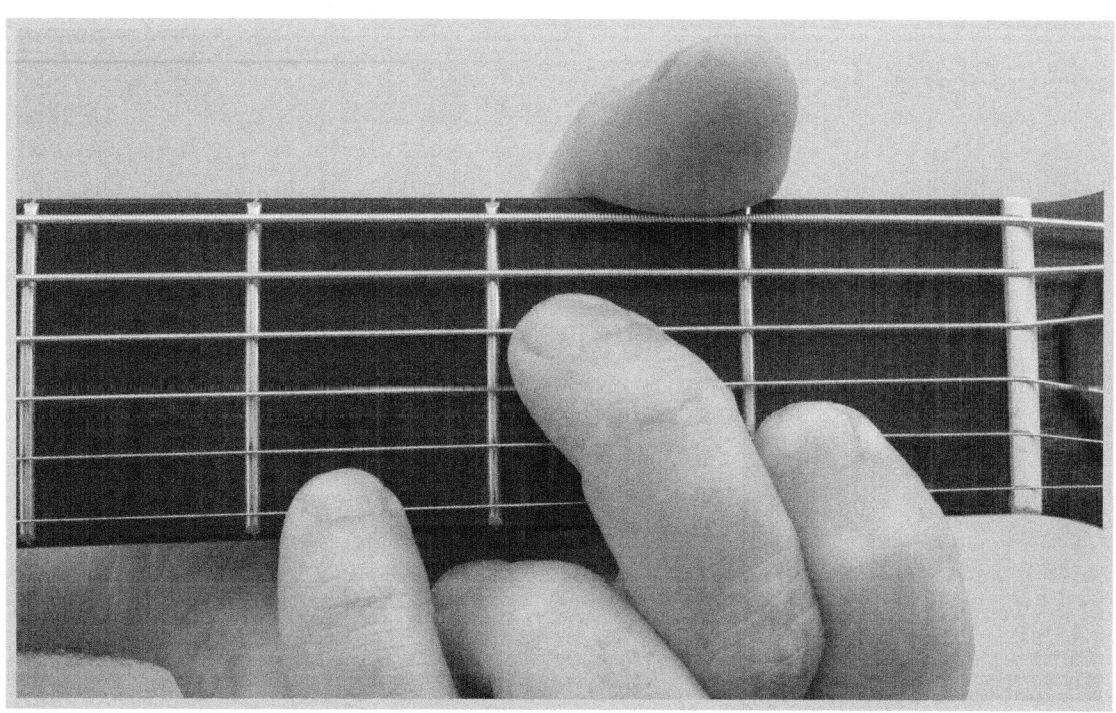

PLAYING EXERCISE

SONG EXAMPLE
Rise - *Gabrielle*

CAPO ON 1ST FRET

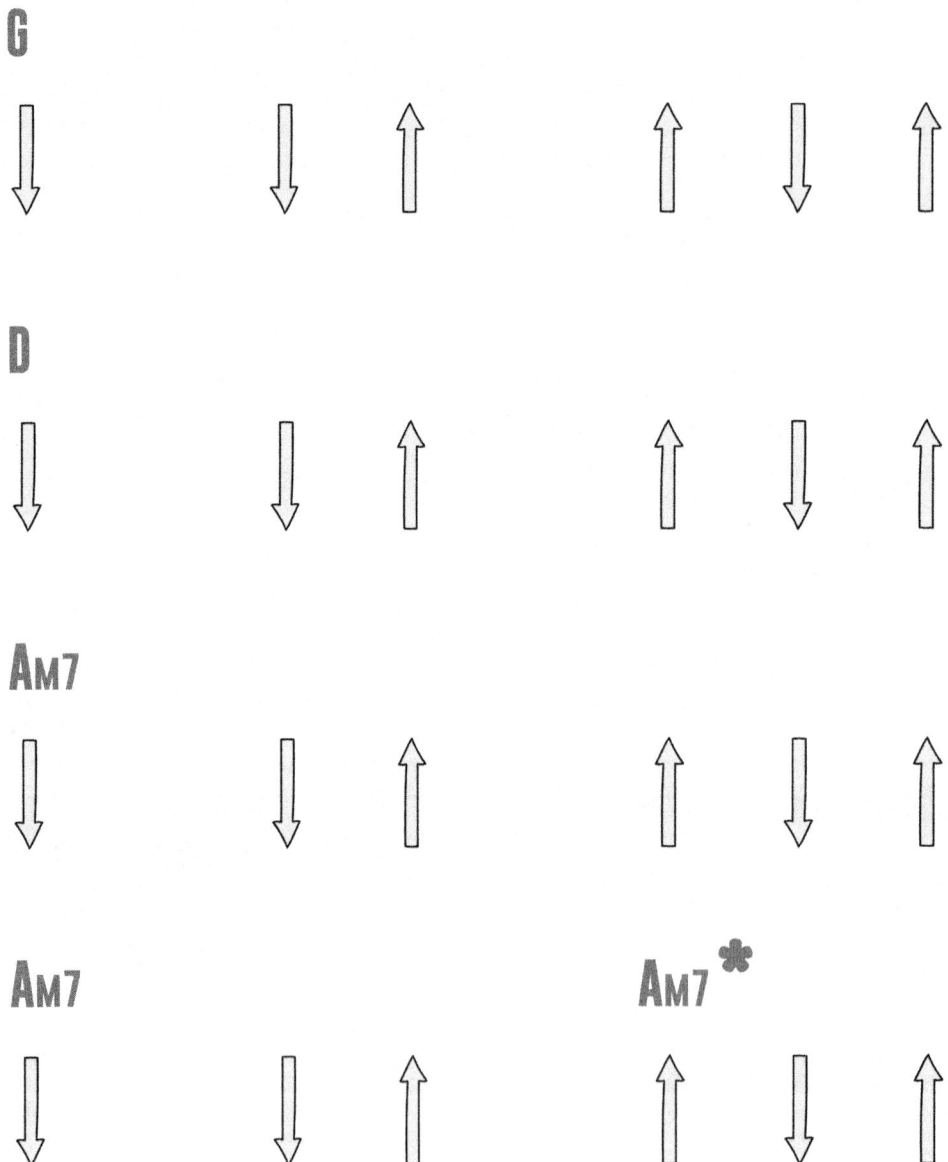

Keep repeating this chord sequence

 **SONG EXAMPLE**   **PLAYING EXERCISE**
Born In The USA - *Bruce Springsteen*

A **4 TIMES**   **CAPO ON 2ND FRET**

D **4 TIMES**

 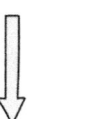   

Keep repeating this chord sequence

SONG EXAMPLE   **PLAYING EXERCISE**
Eleanor Rigby - *The Beatles*

C

Em

Keep repeating this chord sequence

PLAYING EXERCISE

 **SONG EXAMPLE**
Knocking On Heavens Door - *Bob Dylan*

G
↓   ↓   ↓ ↑

D
↓ ↑ ↓ ↑   ↑ ↓ ↑

Am
↓   ↓   ↓ ↑

Am
↓ ↑ ↓ ↑   ↑ ↓ ↑

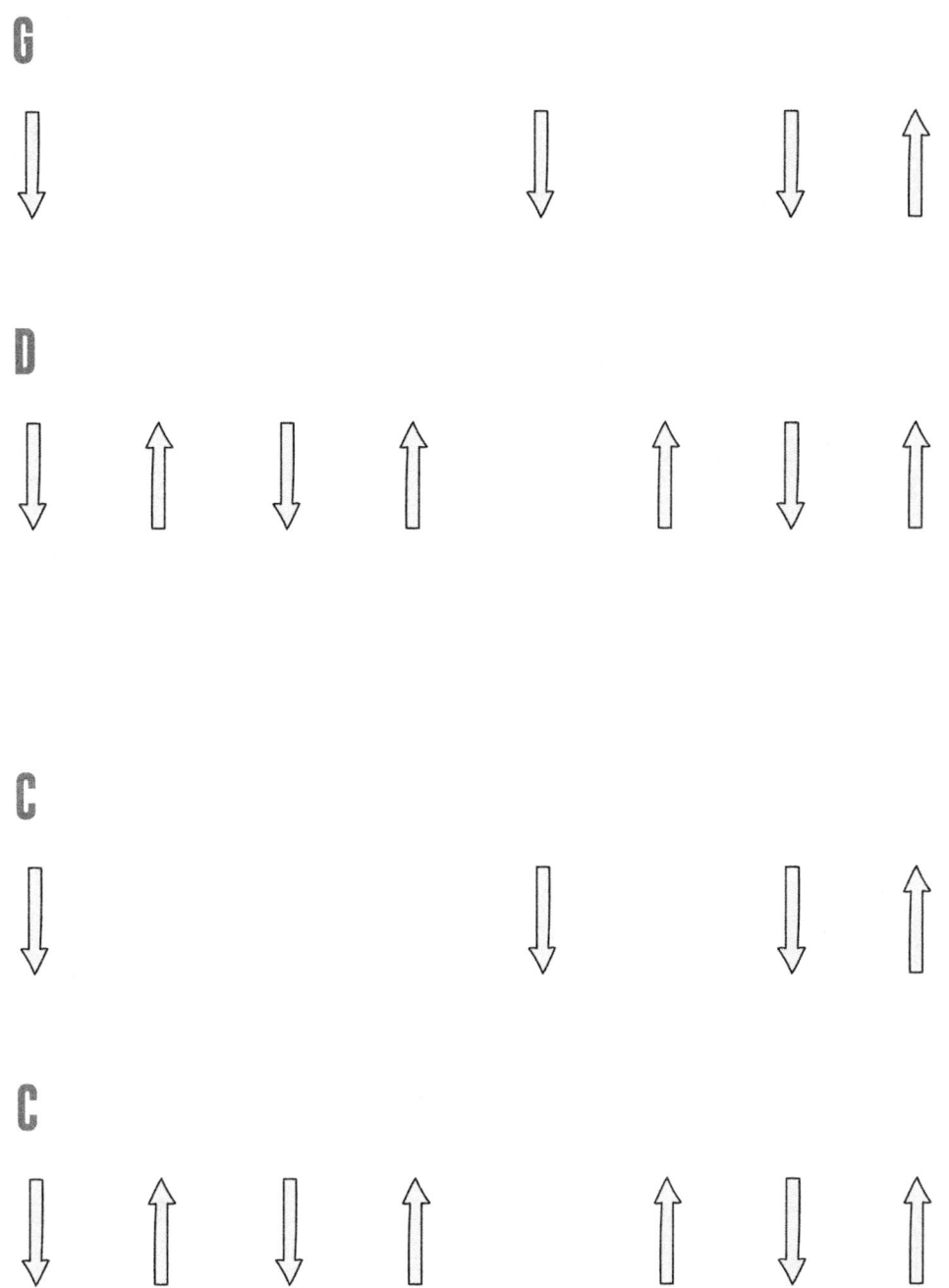

Keep repeating this chord sequence

PLAYING EXERCISE

 SONG EXAMPLE
Sundown - *Gordon Lightfoot*

CAPO ON 2ND FRET

E

E

B7

E

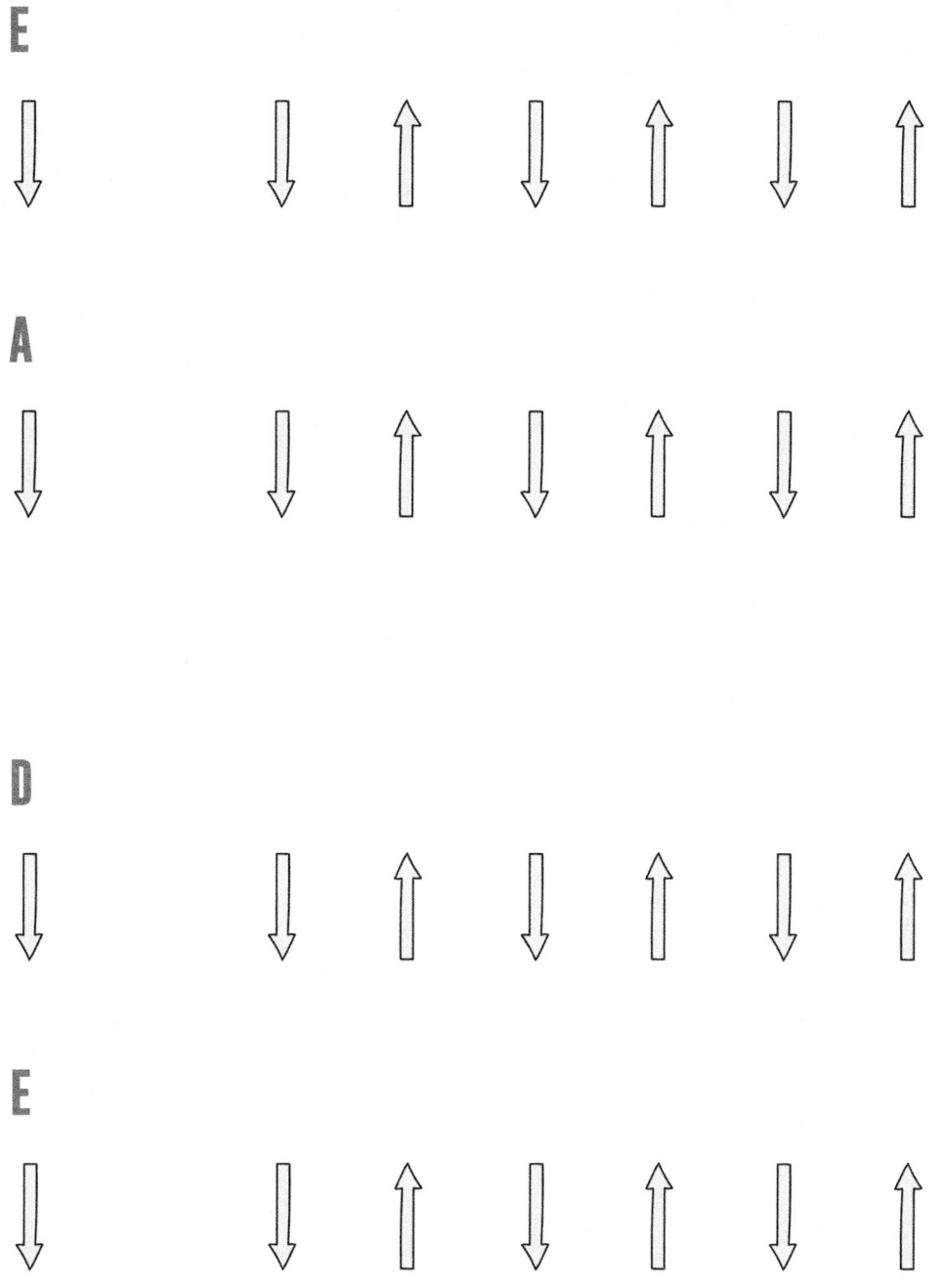

Keep repeating this chord sequence

PLAYING EXERCISE

SONG EXAMPLE
Linger - The Cranberries

D

  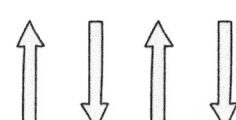  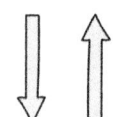

D

  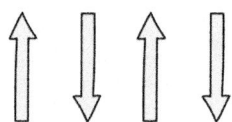  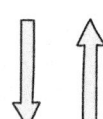

Asus4

  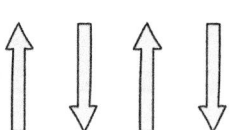  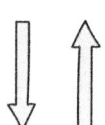

Asus4

  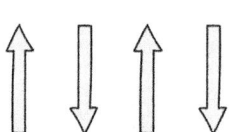  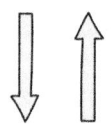

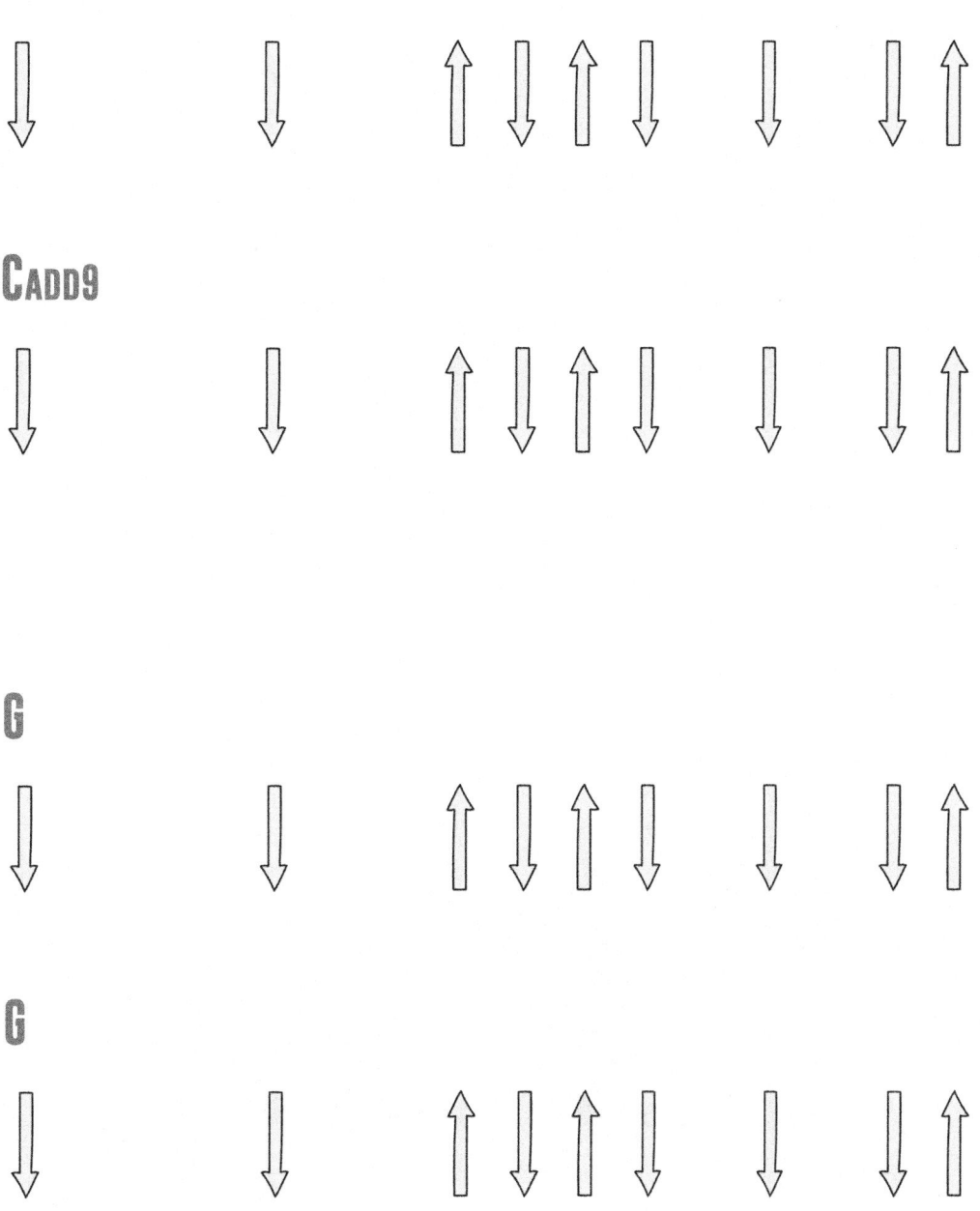

Keep repeating this chord sequence

MORE ABOUT G CHORD

Many great guitarists also play G this way. It frees their 1st and 2nd fingers to add polychords, ornamentation, and bass runs, that are just not possible with the standard G chord.

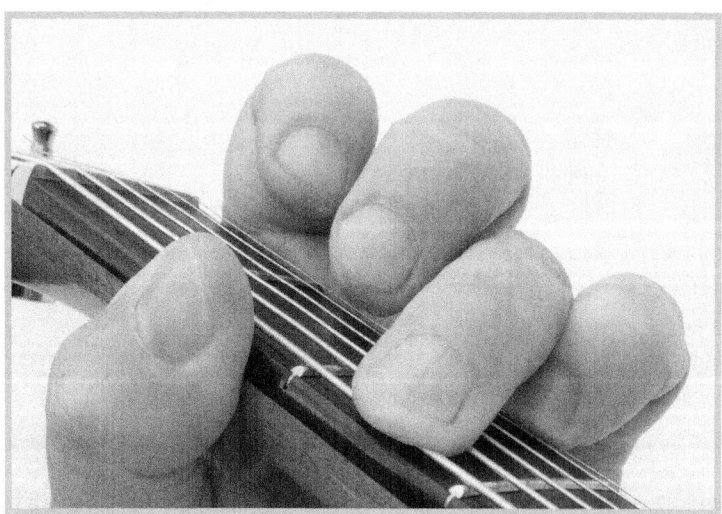

1st and 2nd fingers always close to the fretboard

It is more difficult to learn, but only for a few weeks. As well as giving you many more musical options, playing G this way makes chord changing easier too. ***The possibilities are endless!!!***

G — ANOTHER WAY

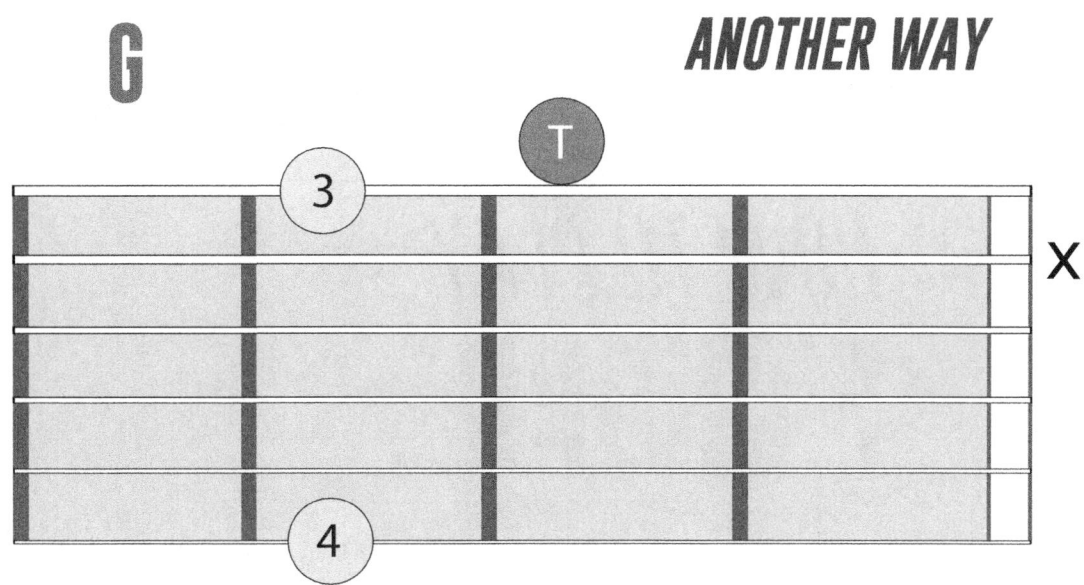

- Thumb may or may not touch 6th string
- 5th string muted by inside of 3rd finger
- Strum 6 strings - Only 5 sound

HOW TO PLAY F CHORD

Many people spend a lifetime struggling with F chord on guitar. There are two reasons for this. Firstly, It requires a completely different hand position to all other guitar chords.

Also, it's often the first chord where learners need to press two strings with one finger. To do this, the palm of your hand must go ***In And Up*** behind the guitar neck; unless you play a barre chord F.

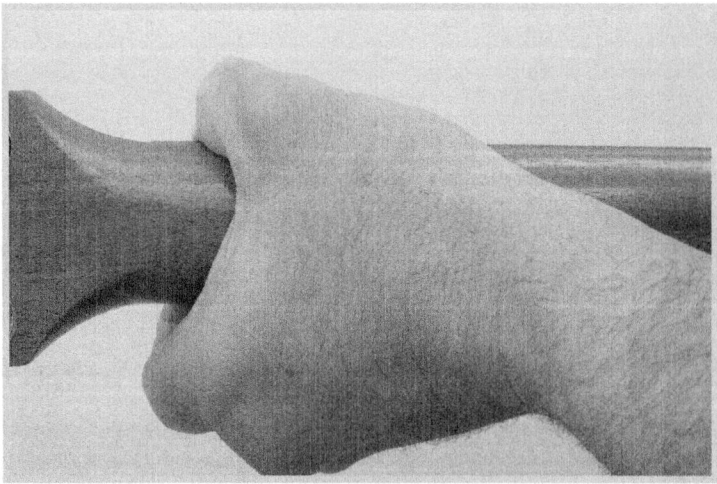

GRAB the guitar neck firmly

Look Behind The Guitar Neck. Try grabbing the guitar, with your thumb over the 6th string. At the same time, move your fingers into the F chord position, with the ***Thumb Rolling Sideways.***

F

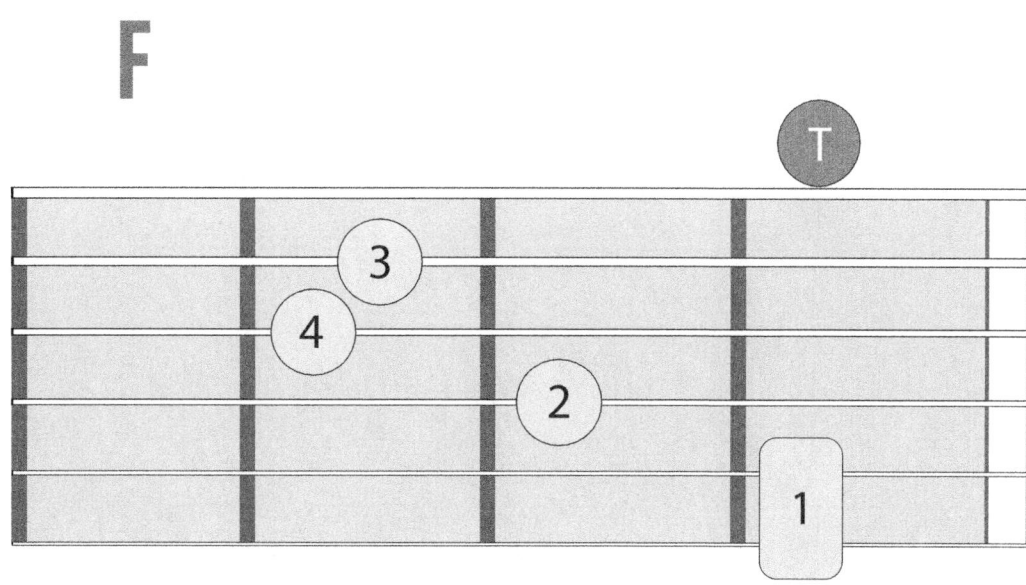

- Grab the guitar neck
- Thumb touching 6th string to mute it
- Strum 6 strings - Only 5 sound

PLAYING EXERCISE

SONG EXAMPLE
Just The Way You Are
Bruno Mars

CAPO ON 5TH FRET

C
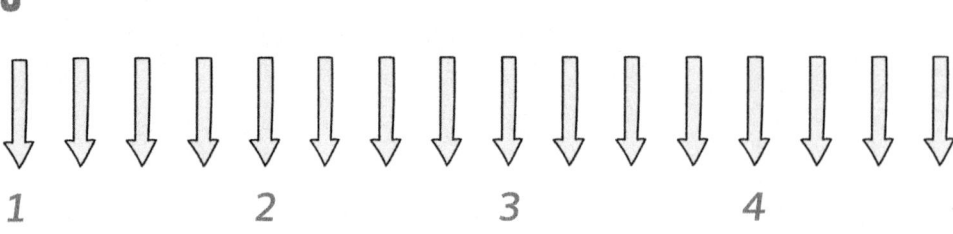

1   2   3   4

Am
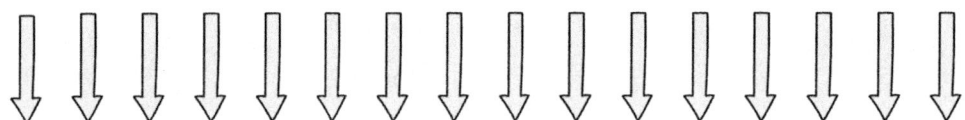

F
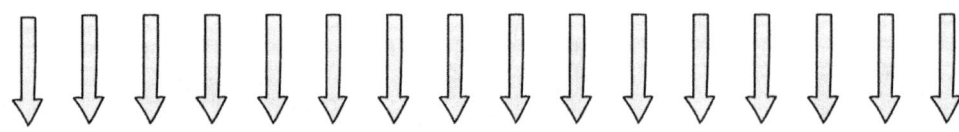

C
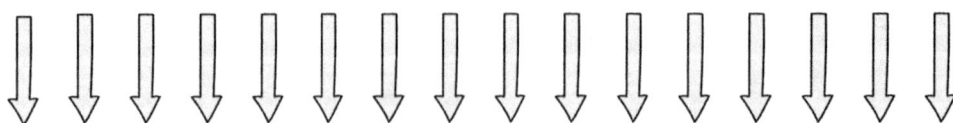

Keep repeating this chord sequence

PLAYING EXERCISE

SONG EXAMPLE
Fishermans Blues - *The Waterboys*

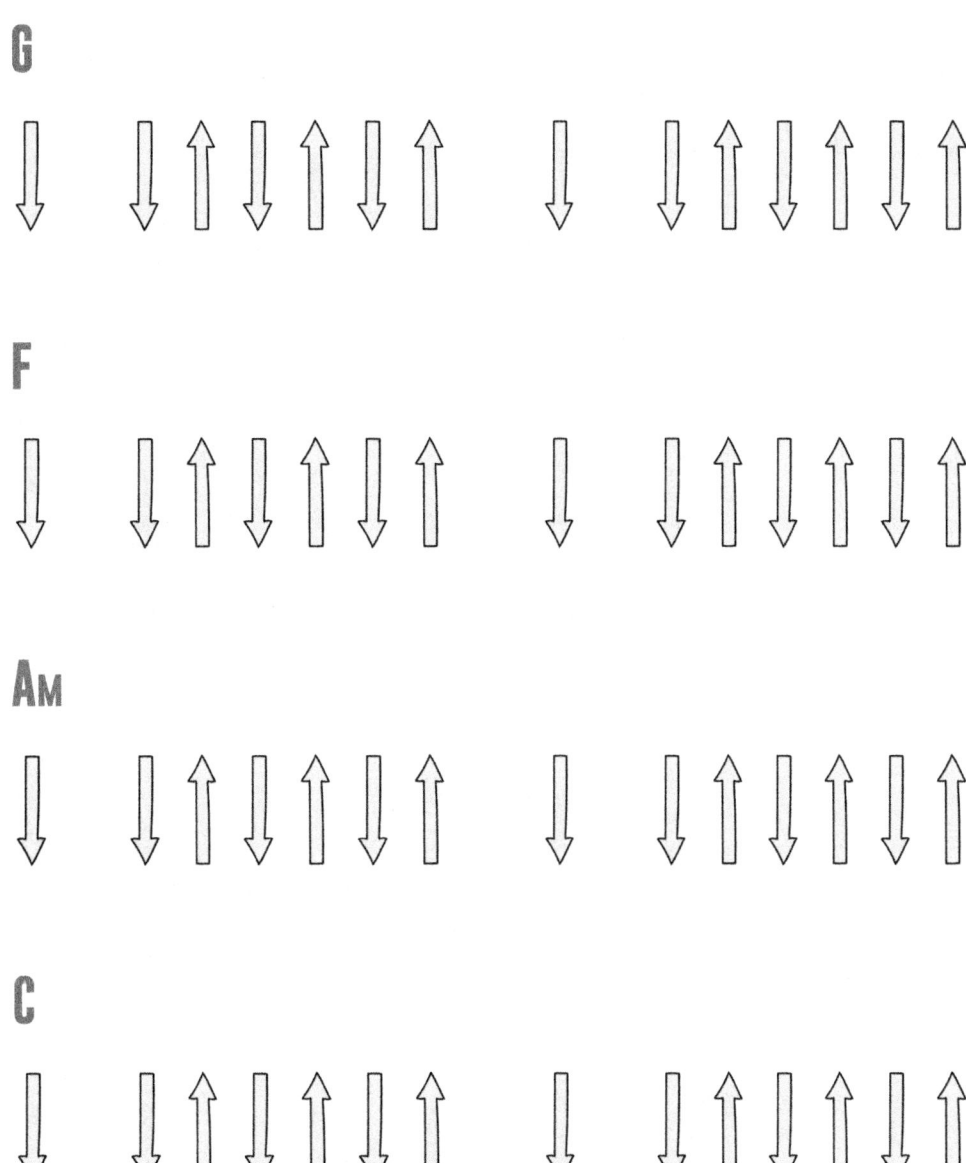

Keep repeating this chord sequence

PLAYING EXERCISE

SONG EXAMPLE
Dreams - Fleetwood Mac

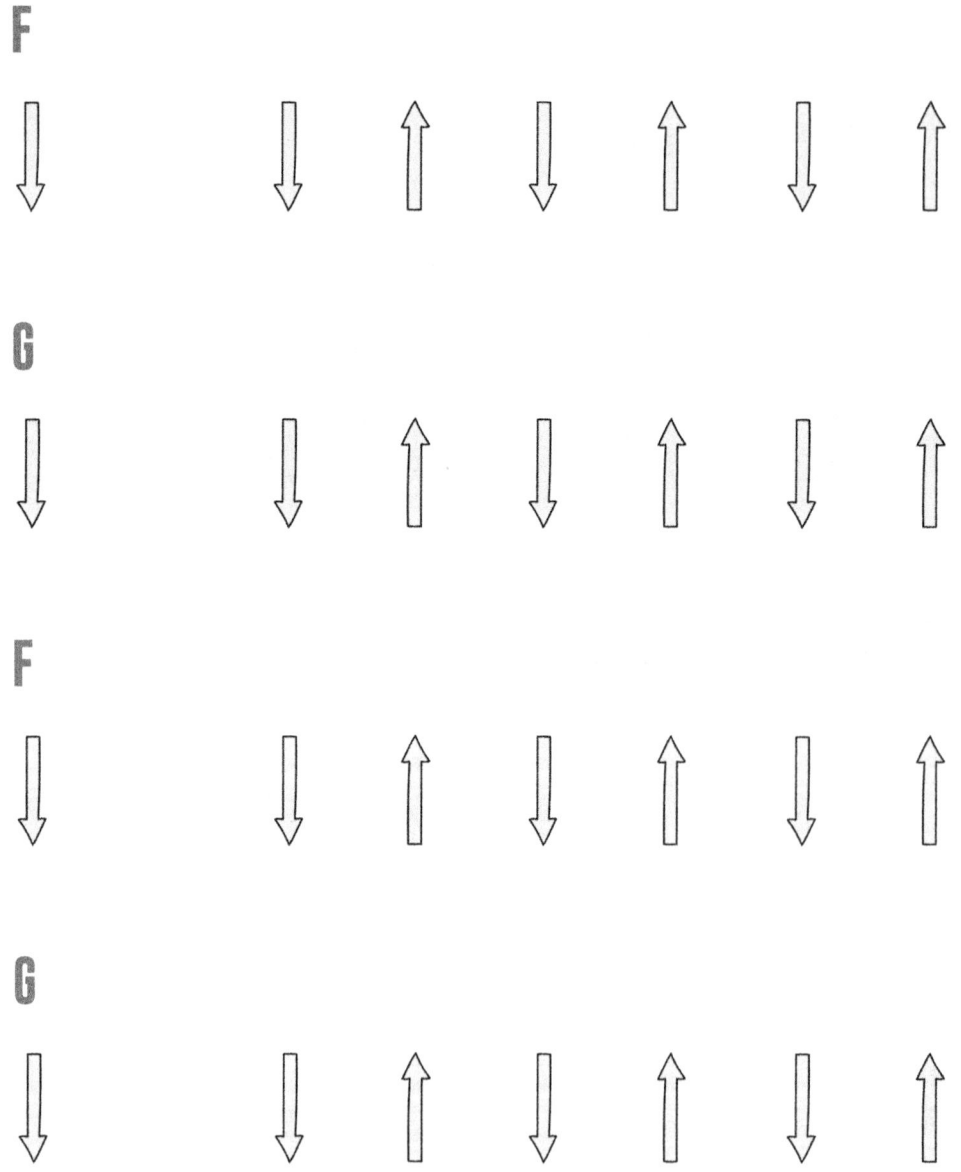

Keep repeating this chord sequence

PLAYING EXERCISE

SONG EXAMPLE
La Bamba - *Ritchie Valens*

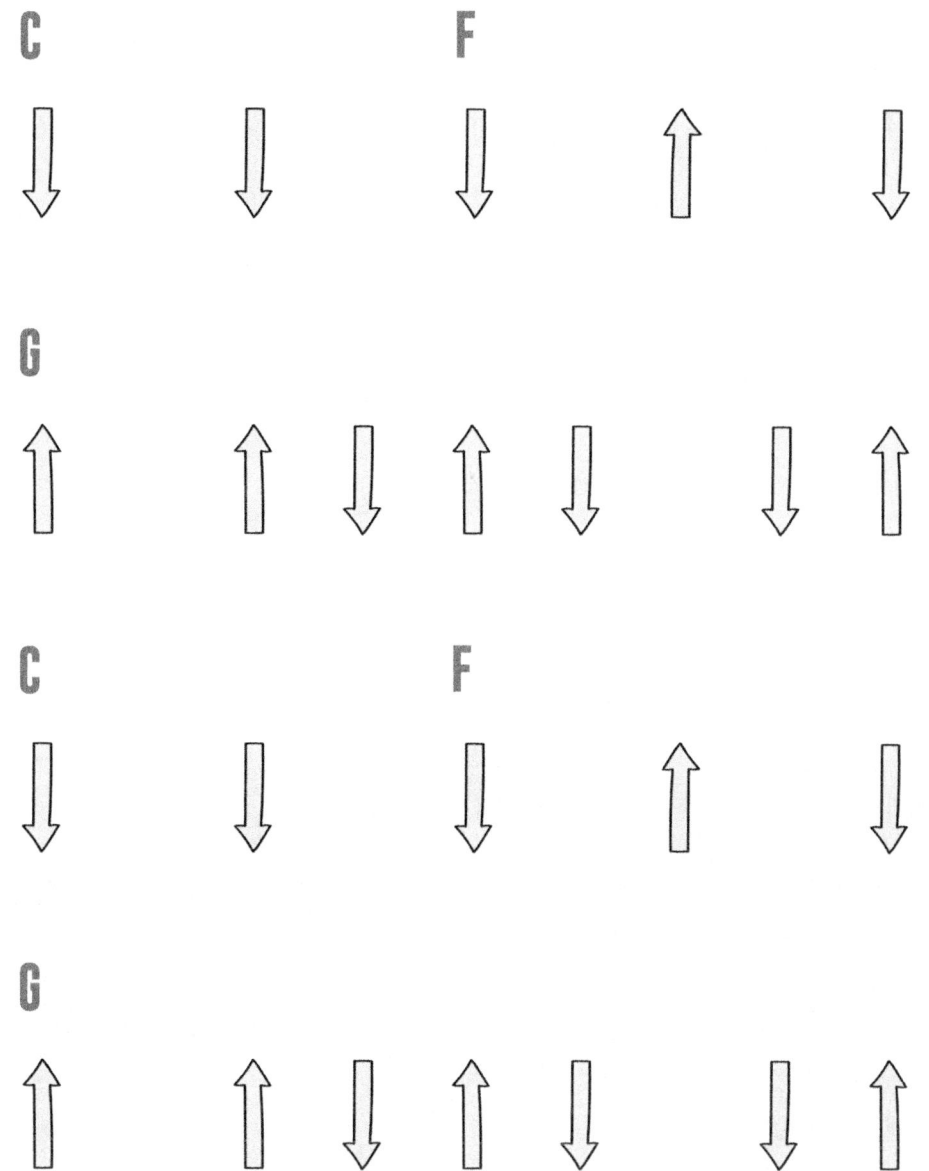

Keep repeating this chord sequence

Dm

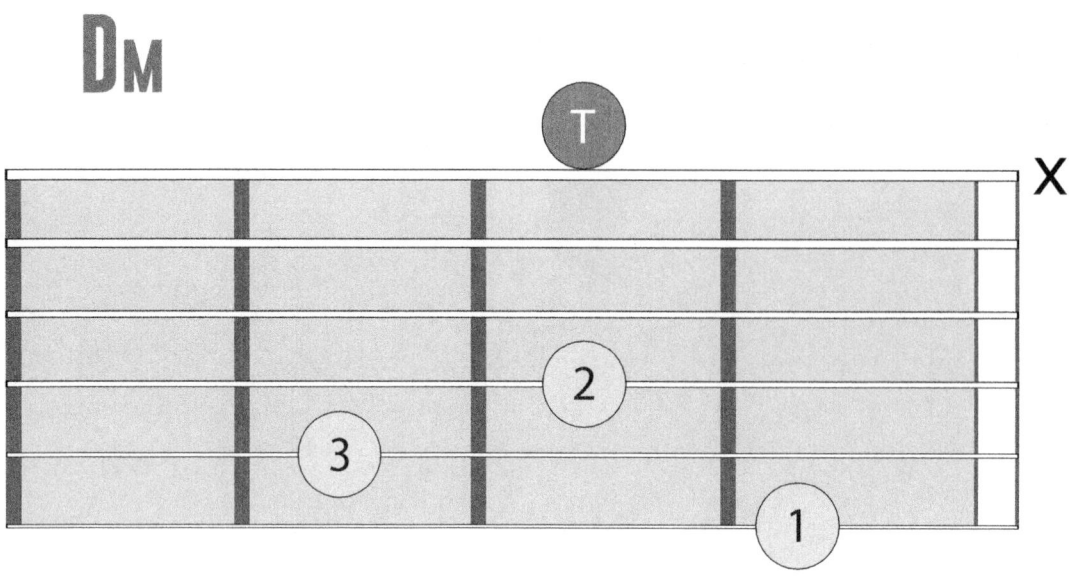

- Thumb touching 6th string
- 3rd finger in middle of fret
- Strum 6 strings - Only 5 sound

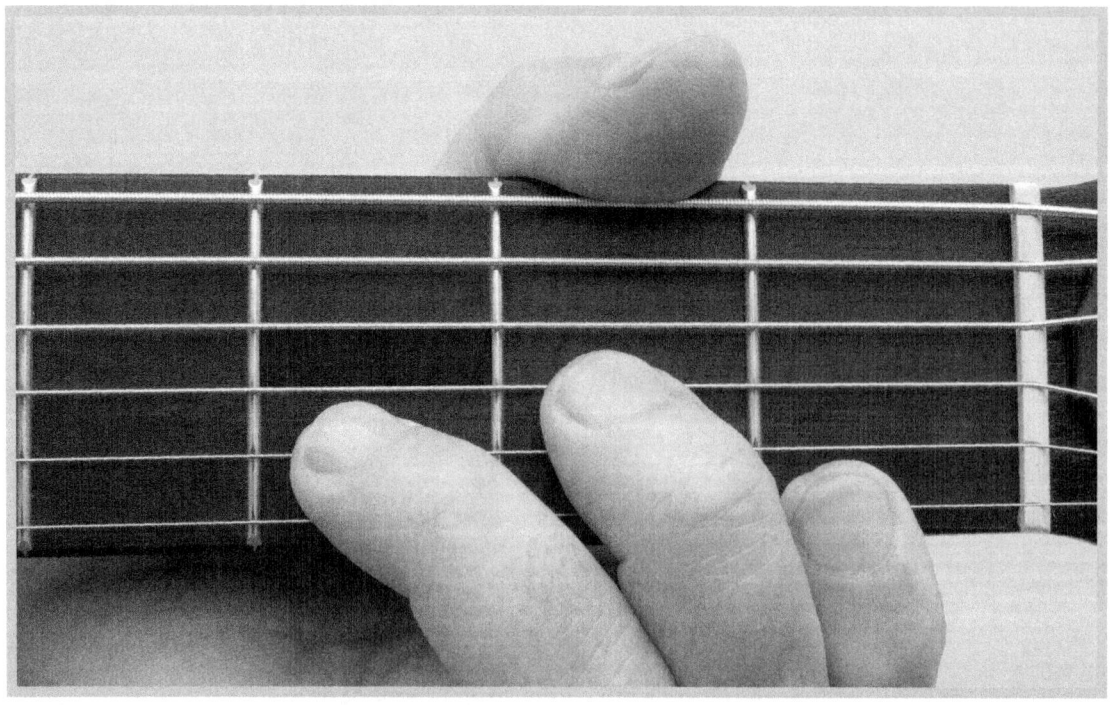

C/B

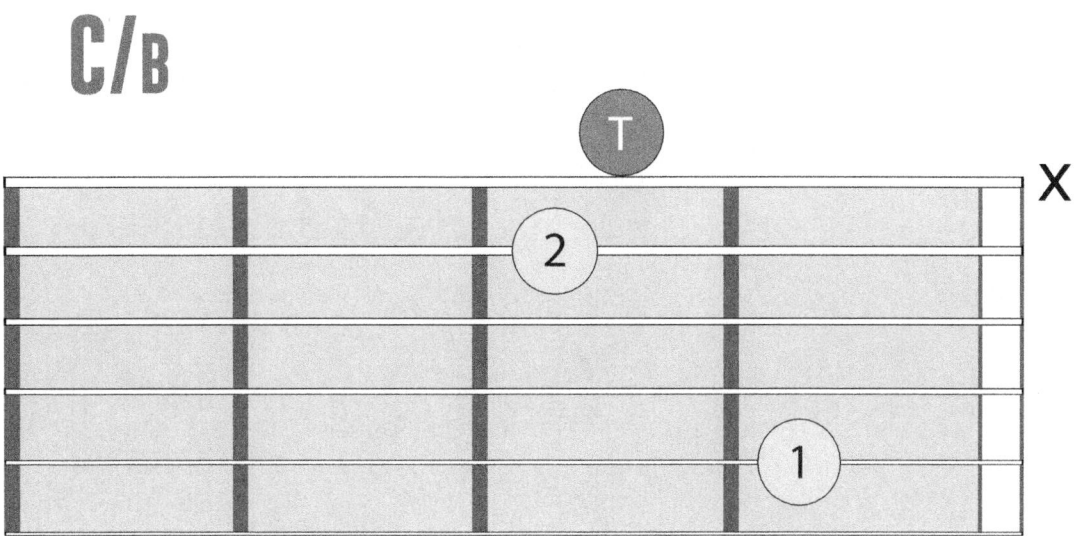

- Thumb touching 6th string
- 1st finger in corner of fret
- Strum 6 strings - Only 5 sound

PLAYING EXERCISE

SONG EXAMPLE
Dancing In The Moonlight - *Toploader*

CAPO ON 3RD FRET

Dm

↓ ↓ ↓ ↑ ↓ ↑

G

↓ ↓ ↓ ↑ ↓ ↑

C   　　　　　**C/B**

↓ ↓ ↓ ↑ ↓ ↑

Am

↓ ↓ ↓ ↑ ↓ ↑

Keep repeating this chord sequence

PLAYING EXERCISE

SONG EXAMPLE
Dancing In The Moonlight - *Thin Lizzy*

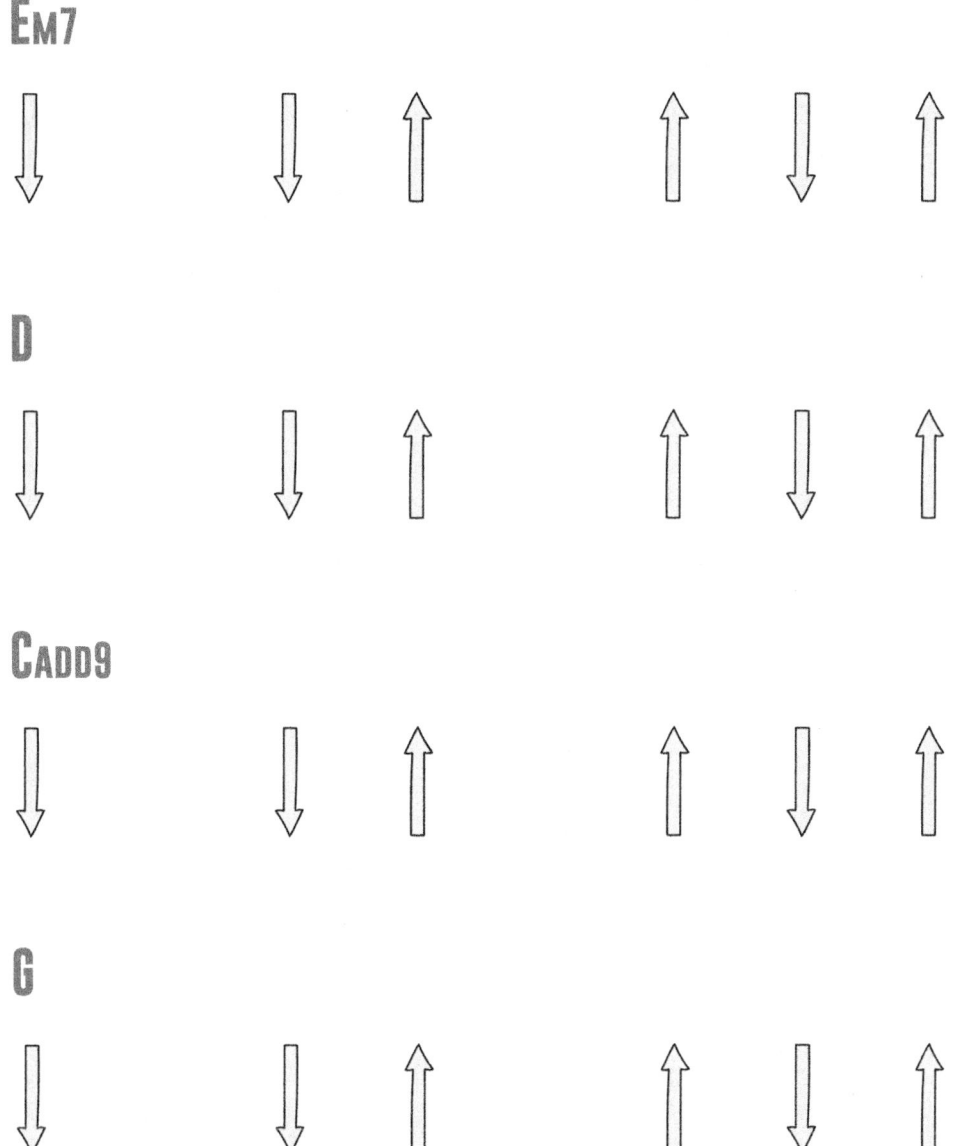

Keep repeating this chord sequence

PLAYING EXERCISE

 SONG EXAMPLE
Last Christmas - *Wham*

CAPO ON 2ND FRET

C

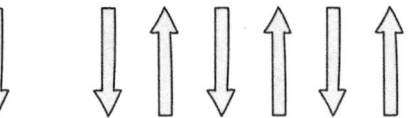 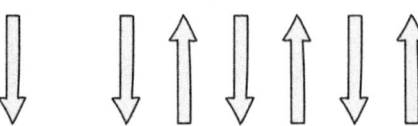

Am

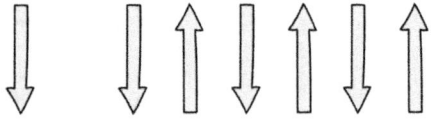 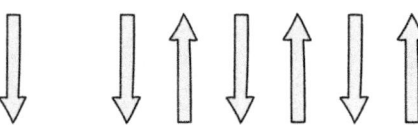

Dm

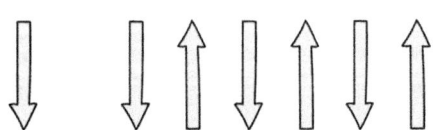 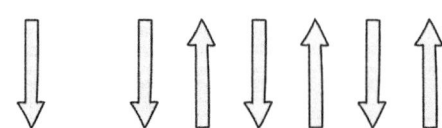

G

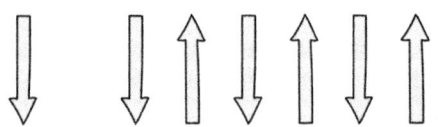 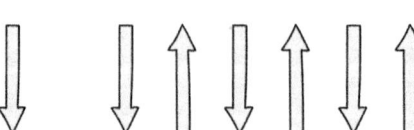

Keep repeating this chord sequence

PLAYING EXERCISE

SONG EXAMPLE
Bitter Sweet Symphony
The Verve

CAPO ON 2ND FRET

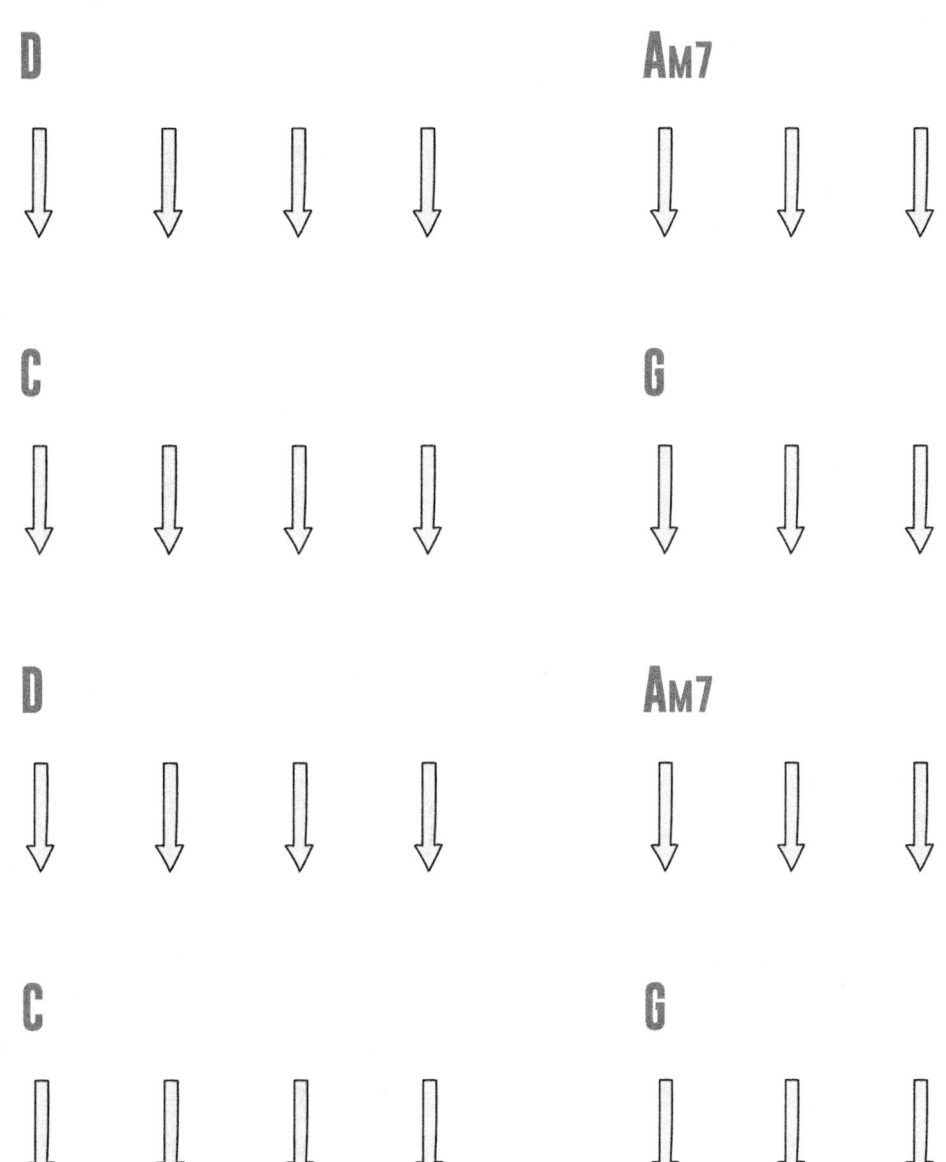

Keep repeating this chord sequence

PLAYING EXERCISE

SONG EXAMPLE
Jammin - *Bob Marley*

CAPO ON 2ND FRET

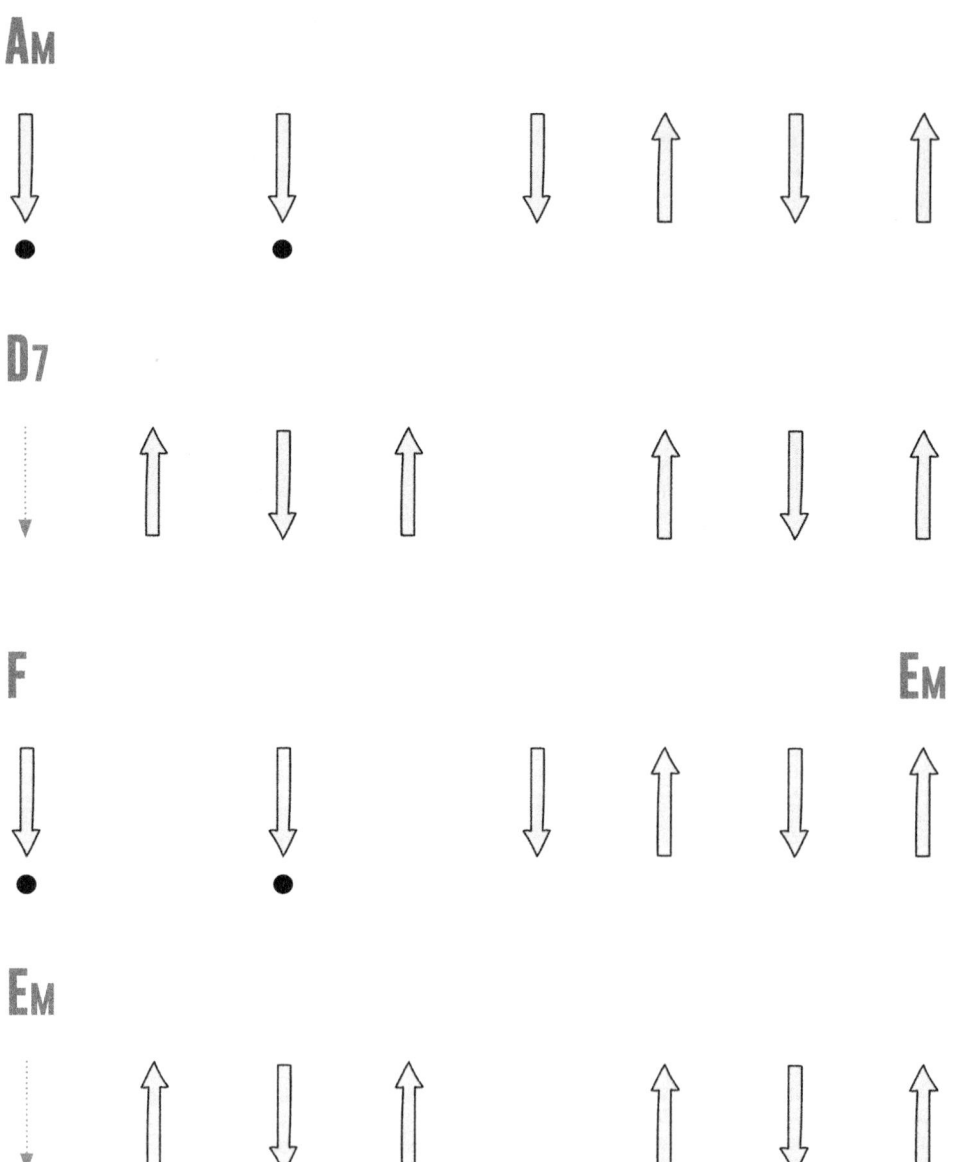

Keep repeating this chord sequence

PLAYING EXERCISE

 **SONG EXAMPLE**
Back To Black
Amy Winehouse

CAPO ON 5TH FRET

Am
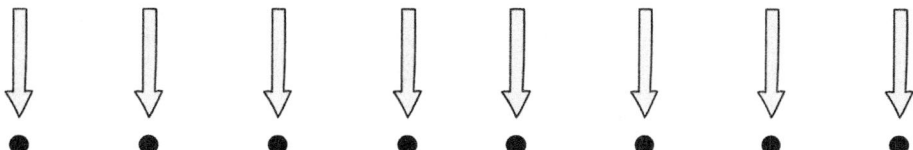

Dm
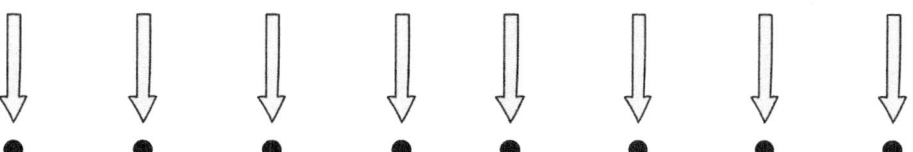

F
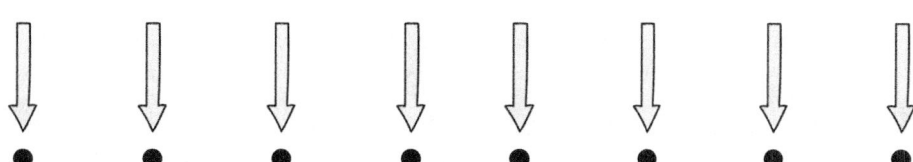

E
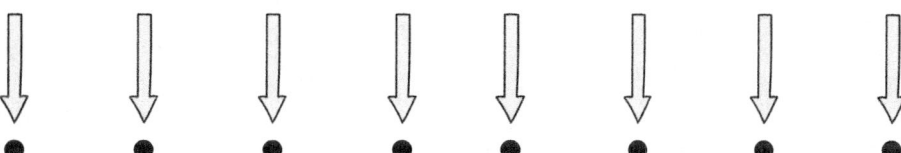

Keep repeating this chord sequence

Dmaj7

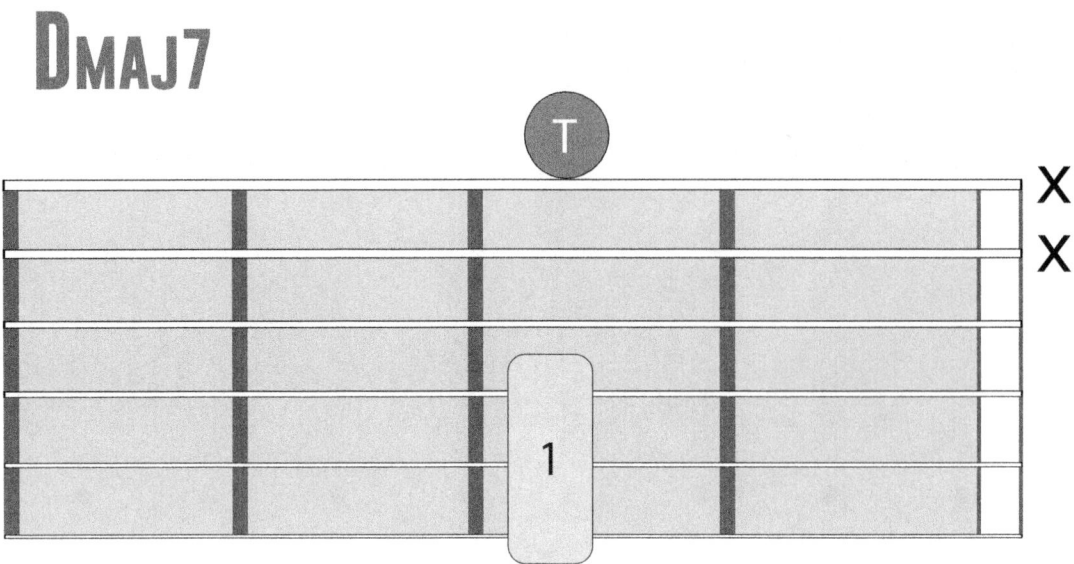

- Sometimes played instead of D
- 1st finger pressing 3 strings
- Strum bottom 4 strings

E$_M$7

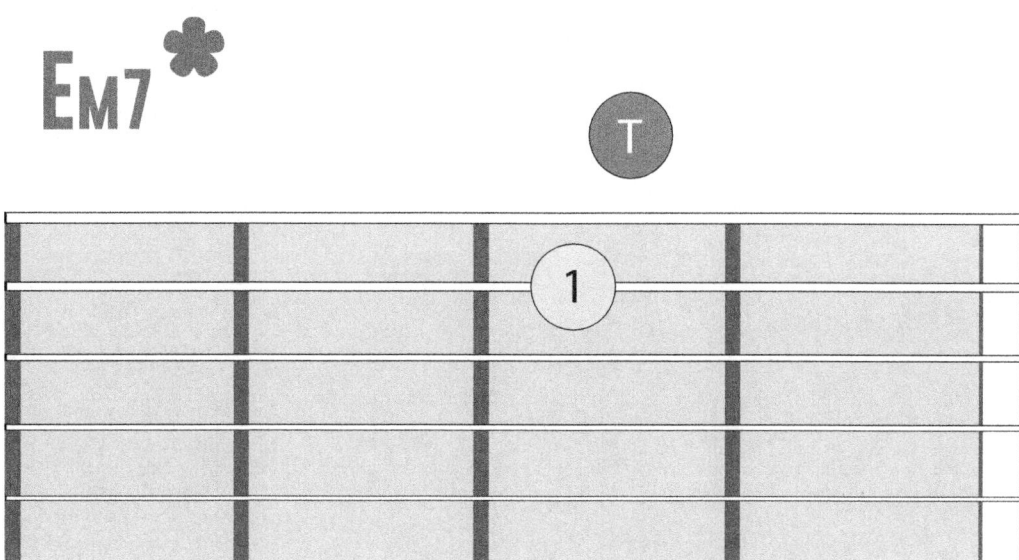

- Thumb not touching 6th string
- Also played with 2nd finger
- All 6 strings sound

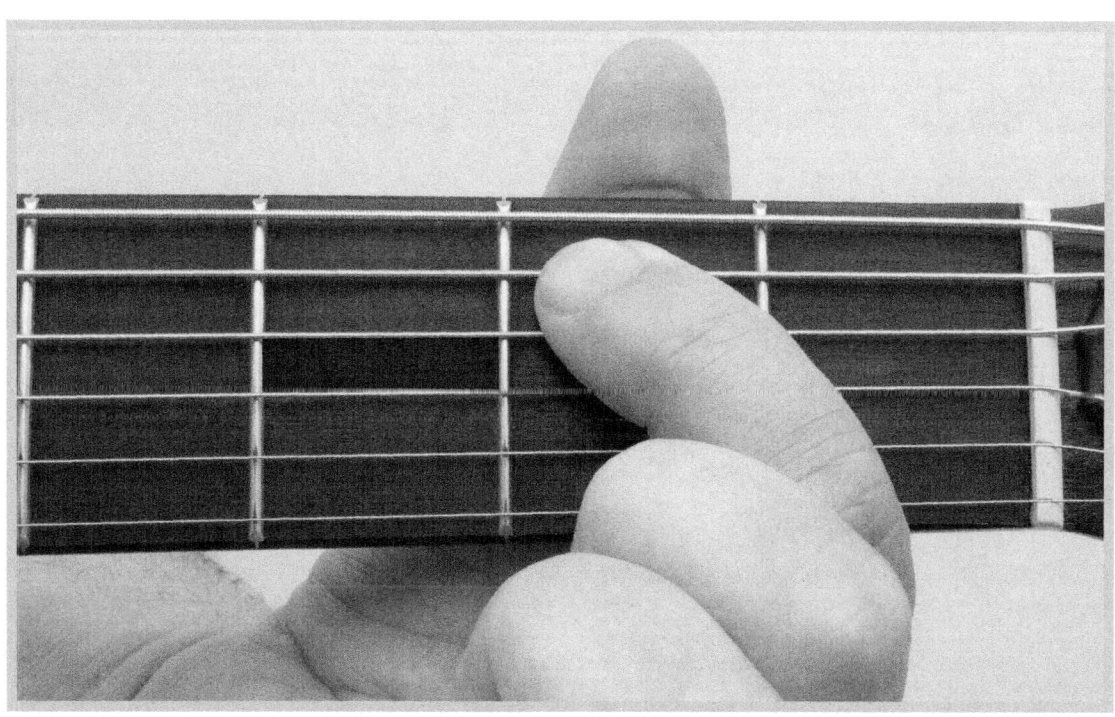

PLAYING EXERCISE

 SONG EXAMPLE
Make It With You - Bread

CAPO ON 2ND FRET

DMAJ7

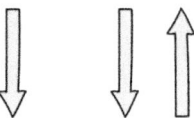  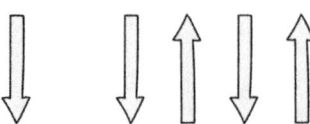

EM7 *

 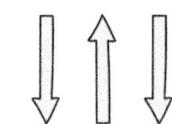  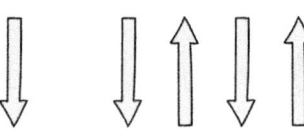

DMAJ7

 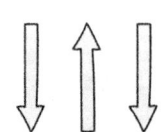   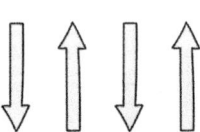

EM7 *

 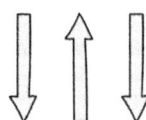   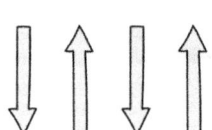

Keep repeating this chord sequence

PLAYING EXERCISE

SONG EXAMPLE
Albatross - *Fleetwood Mac*

CAPO ON 2ND FRET

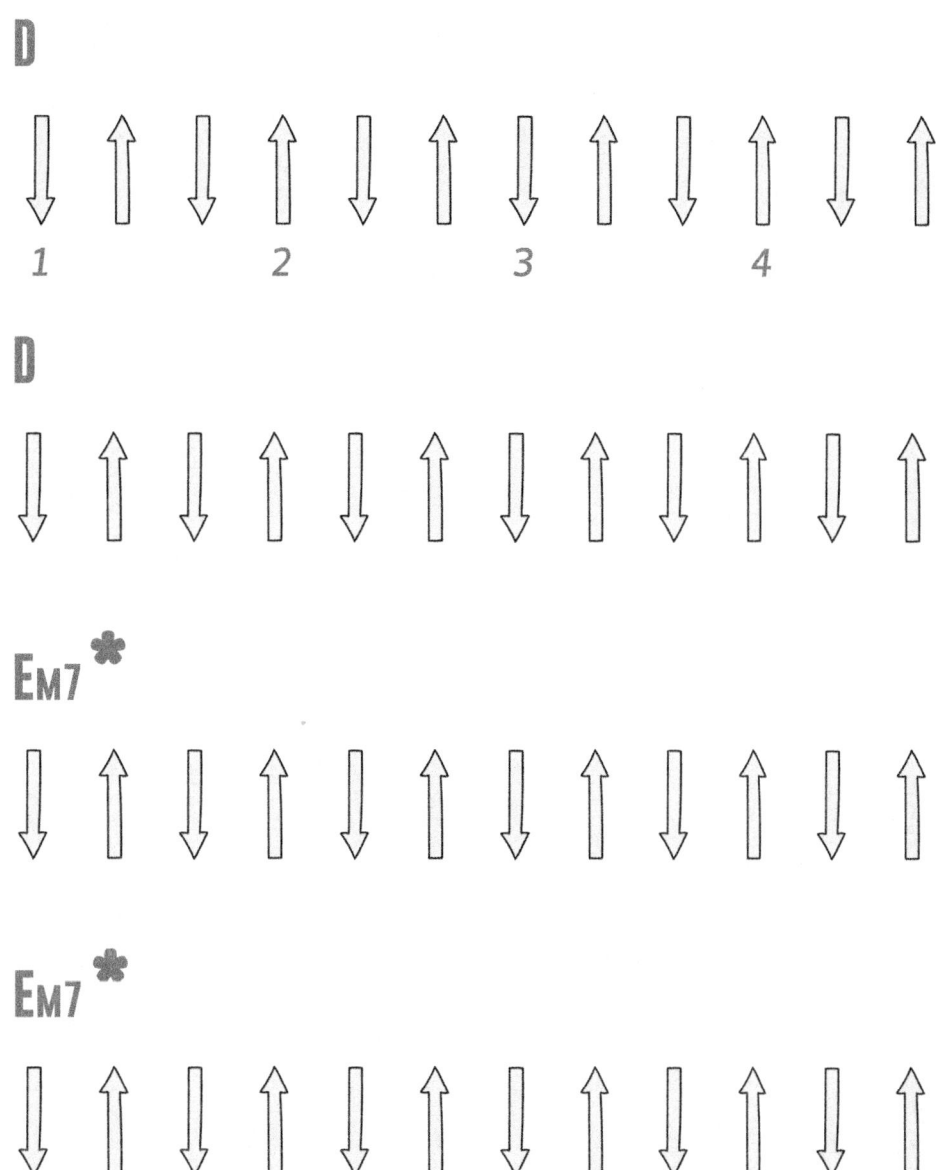

Keep repeating this chord sequence

CHORD INDEX

A

A	92
Am	53
Am7	98
Am7*	99
Asus2	63
Asus4	68

B

B7	91

C

C	62
C/B	117
Cmaj7	26
Cadd9	42
Cadd9*	43

D	D	41
	Dm	116
	Dsus2	61
	D7	54
	Dmaj7	124
E	E	90
	Em	25
	Em7	60
	Em7*	125
	E7sus4	29
F	F	111
	Fmaj7	55
	F# easy	28
G	G	40
	G another way	109
	G/F#	69
	G6	27

MEET THE AUTHOR

Pauric Mather's ground breaking guitar books and lessons are truly unique. Easily the most individual and personalised you will ever find. They have helped thousands of people to learn guitar. What's even more remarkable is that you need no knowledge of music to learn from his teaching style.

As well as being an expert guitar teacher, Pauric Mather is the author of 4 #1 best sellers.

From Dublin, Ireland, he's been a professional guitarist since 1987, and has worked with many successful artists.

Pauric Mather is now the most translated guitar author in the world. His books and teaching methods are available in more than 10 languages.

Printed in Dunstable, United Kingdom